The Frank and Jesse James Saga

The Beginning of the End for the James Gang

by
R. G. "Jerry" Tidwell

Published by:
Bluewater Publications
1812 CR 111
Killen, Alabama 35645
www.BluewaterPublications.com

Dedication:

Paris Arnold "Billy" Rogers

Michael Finney Gray

This book is dedicated to longtime family friends: Doris and Paris Arnold "Billy" Rogers. Also to my first cousin Michael Finney Gray.

Appreciation:

I would like to express my appreciation to the following people who assisted me in this work:

Cathy Palmer and **Ilena Holder** of the Jackson County Advanced Writer's Group who helped write the play for Chapter 27.

Ronald Pettus who unselfishly loaned his archives to use as source material for the play which is included in Part III.

Dr. Kenneth R. Johnson, Professor Emeritus of History, UNA, who made available some of his original work and gave his approval for its use. Also for his willingness to answer questions posed to him from time to time.

Table of Contents

Part I

The Perils and Pitfalls of Strictly Internet Genealogical Research

R. G. "Jerry" Tidwell
May 2010

Chapter 1

Hot on the Trail of Frank and Jesse James

Billy Rogers and Finney Gray's Family

Take a good look around you at your next gathering of people at any social function or at work. Is there someone sitting near you that shares the same bloodline of Frank and Jesse James? The chances are very good that there is someone and they may not even know it!

In this project I have traced the James pedigree on the internet as far as possible and still be reasonably sure that it was accurate, but did push the envelope in places where noted. The early James family was prolific and there were numerous decedents all through the ages.

This project started off innocently enough. My uncle by marriage, Finney Gray, mentioned to me on several occasions that some family member had traced back his family's lineage and had found that they were related to Frank and Jesse James from his mother's side. Finney said he had documents they had given him but he never showed them to me before he died. I thought they were lost.

Paris A. (Billy) Rogers and Finney Gray are first cousins. Finney's mother, **Mayme Rogers Gray,** and Billy's father, **Ira Norman Rogers,** were brother and sister. While visiting the Shoals area recently, Billy told me that he had a copy of all of this documentation and offered to let me see it when he had time to dig it out. So I went back to Scottsboro which is a little over 100 miles away and Billy started digging.

During the funeral of my youngest brother, Richard Samuel Tidwell, around Labor Day 2009, Billy told me that his grandfather's name was William Joshua Rogers and he came out of **Giles County Tennessee** as a young man. He was orphaned at the age of about one year old, according to Billy, and his grandparents Esther Hicks James and Joshua James had raised him. William Joshua's father died in the Civil War in 1864 and his mother died in August of 1861. Billy has family stories to share with me.

It should be noted at this point just where Giles County Tennessee is in relationship to the Shoals area since it became so essential to this project. It is just north of the Alabama state line with Lawrence County Tennessee to the west and Lincoln County Tennessee to the east. Cities and towns in Giles County include Pulaski, Ardmore and Minor Hill as well as many other communities.

From myths and deeds attributed to Frank and Jesse James and documented facts, they did indeed spend a good deal of time in the Shoals area of North Alabama. It has long been reported that they were visiting with family members.

I decided at this point to do a strictly internet genealogical research project to see if enough information could be generated to tie in the Rogers family and the James family from information on the internet. I always use Familysearch.org for a macro search to tie in the broad picture and then try to refine the details from various family trees on Ancestry.com.

I had about two weeks to pursue this project on the internet to see if enough information could be located to start an internet search and tie everything together. I knew full well going into this that the information listed on the internet is only as accurate as the research the person does who enters it and how accurately they type. There are a lot of inconsistencies and confusing things listed there. One must pick up enough information to sort it all out. I realized that the information gathered would probably not be enough to support the claim that the families were related or to reach the conclusion that they were not.

The goals of this project were as follows:

Pick up supporting documentation from other internet sources other than Familysearch.org and Ancestry.com offered by people who have done conventional research and have reported it on the internet.

Do only internet research to see how it compares with what Billy and Finney's relatives had done.

Trace all pertinent family trees back as far as possible on the internet.

And lastly, see if there was a connection between the Rogers family and the family of Frank and Jesse James.

Little did I realize at the time that two weeks would not even be enough for me to even scratch the surface of this project. This soon became a very time consuming and lengthy project! Especially trying to tie everything together and edit. This project ended up taking nine full months of most of my spare time and all of my waking hours toward the end. It may take six more months to publish.

I soon ran into problems. It soon became evident that there were apparently two William Joshua Rogers that were born about the same time or were confused on the internet. Both died about the same time. I later found a third one and have separated them into three scenarios and will try to use Billy's family stories to see if we can chose the most plausible one.

These different scenarios claim different parents for William Joshua Rogers but pick him up as a common ancestor of Ira Norman Rogers and Mayme Esther Rogers Gray.

Chapter 2

Much is written about the family and exploits of Frank and Jesse James. About the best one that could be found on the internet was **"The Outlaws"** by the late **James W. Sames III** April 11, 1921-December 23, 2005.

This is the most complete source about the early family genealogy, family life, Civil War experiences and their life as outlaws and its aftermath that I could locate out of all the sources available. It is well written and a must for any Frank and Jesse James inquiry and was the most complete source available for this work.

Only the information on Frank and Jesse James from this referenced source was used early on and this is where I obtained many of the leads that allowed me to do genealogical research on the internet.

It is well worth pulling up and reading online or printing for even a casual look at the James Brothers.

There is supplemental research and additions by Michael Graves who now owns the copyright.

"The Outlaws" is summarized as follows:

Mr. Sames starts his work with this description as he states:

Not since the days of the noted English highwayman Robin Hood and his merry men has an outlaw captured the imagination of the public, as the hard-riding, straight-shooting bank and train robbers, Frank and Jesse James and their bushwhacking band of outlaws. They are perhaps the most famous robbers of the old West, not excluding Kentucky. In Missouri their birthplace is a state monument, the only one for any outlaw. They gave the nation its first peacetime bank robbery and perfected train robbing, the first was on August 7, 1863. The Liberty, Missouri Tribune, a pro-Union newspaper, carried the following item:

"Three Southern Gentlemen In Search Of Their Rights-On the morning of the 6th of August, Frank James with two other companions, stopped David Mitchell, on the road to Leavenworth, about 6 miles west of Liberty, and took from him $1.25, his pocket knife, and a pass he had from the Provost Marshal to cross the plains. This is one of the rights these men are fighting for. James sent his compliments to Major Green, and said he would like to see him."

Such was the first recorded robbery committed by Frank James. During the next two decades he, his brother Jesse, and their sidekicks, the Younger brothers, became America's most famous outlaws. Today, a century after Jesse's murder and Frank's surrender in 1882, they still possess that distinction. Here is the story of their rise to fame, along with the sometimes brutal facts: facts which have been concealed by legends, like a bandit's face by a mask.

Mr. Sames next goes into details about the father and mother of Frank and Jesse James as he states:

Frank and Jesse James father, Robert Sallee James was born July 17, 1818 in Logan County Kentucky, a place called Lickskillet on the Whippoorwill Creek. He died August 18, 1850 near Placerville El Dorado California. He was the son of John and Mary Poore James, both natives of Virginia, but very early settlers of Logan County, Kentucky. Robert was one of nine children, five sons and four daughters. The five sons were as follows: Wm. James (1811), John James (1815), Robert S. James (1818), Thomas M. James (1823), Drury Woodson James (1825); Mary James (1809) m John Mimms, Elizabeth James (1816) m Tillman West, Nancy James (1830) m George Hite, Mary Elizabeth James (1827) m John R. (Hugh) Cohorn. Mary Elizabeth's mother, Mary (Poore) James died the following day after she was born. A neighbor, Mary Elizabeth Hendricks (who had lost her child one week before), breast fed the new infant girl a few weeks until she became very healthy and continued to raise her as her own until she was married. The name "Mary Elizabeth" came from three sources, the names of her two older sisters, so she may always remember them, her mother, Mary and her godmother's name, Mary Elizabeth Hendricks who raised her to adulthood. (Facts obtained from the old Hendrick-Newton Bible, on record at the James Museum, Kearney, MO.)

Robert S. James graduated from Georgetown College, having completed all requirements of the four-year classical course, on June 29, 1843. His degree was the Bachelor of Arts. According to faculty records, final examination for the senior class was taken on May 24, 1843. Robert is listed as having tied for third place honors in the class. For his accomplishment, he was awarded the opportunity to present an oration at the commencement exercises. All associates who knew him spoke of him as a kindly man of God. So convincing as a Minister one would remember his sermons the rest of their life. He was an educator, gifted orator, and a successful farmer.

While attending Georgetown College, at a church function, Robert met Zerelda Cole. Zerelda was attending St. Catherine's Female School in Lexington. In May 1840, Robert in his studies at the seminary was encouraged to attend a meeting where a group of young people of different faiths was present. There he could see how he handled himself. He lectured at St. Catherine's and tried to convert the girls. One girl in particular seemed to respond to his every word, and he soon found out she was Baptist. Soon after they met, they started seeing each other and attended other Baptist Church functions. It is said, Stamping Ground Baptist Church is where they most often met.

By the time school ended in the spring of 1841 they were not speaking. Most young men in those days had strong beliefs that a woman should be silent and not express their political thoughts. Zerelda was of the Cole and Lindsay Families, who had been famous for their courageous deeds during the Revolutionary War. She inherited these same traits, and with her education it made her unwilling to comply with his wishes. But three days later before fall 1841, the desire and love for Zerelda was too strong, Robert proposed to her. Robert and Zerelda were married December 28, 1841 at the home of her Uncle Judge James Madison Lindsay, in Stamping Ground, Kentucky. The house is still standing and presently owned by Marguerite Sprague on Locust Fork Pike, Scott County.

Zerelda was dismissed from the Stamping Ground Baptist Church on the fourth Saturday in February 1842. In August 1842, the young couple made a journey through the semi-wilderness to visit her mother Sarah, and her step-dad Robert Thomason in Clay County, Missouri. Robert James, with a sad heart, returned to Georgetown College, leaving alone his pregnant wife with her mother. His desire was to finish his final year of theological training and return home by next Christmas, but the Missouri River was frozen the poor roads were treacherous, so it was spring after he had graduated before he arrived at Kearney, to reunite with his wife and a new son born January 10, 1843, Alexander Franklin James. He later returned to Georgetown College in 1848 where he received his Master's Degree. He then decided to settle in Clay County where he purchased a farm from Asa W. Thomason, near Centerville, a town which later changed its name to Kearney. The farm had no house and they built a cabin during the next spring. Robert bought two slaves.

He then began to farm and to preach and was good at both. His other children are as follow: Jesse James was born 1847; Susan in 1849 and Robert only lived 1 month. Robert S. James lived in Missouri for about eight years. During that time the minister's farming supported them. In a volume of records about religious activity in Western Missouri between the years 1842-1850, Maple and Rider, have this to say about the Reverend James' ministry:

"The influence of this pioneer toward the Baptist cause in Western Missouri is not measured by the length of time for which he entered into all enterprises that worked towards the building up of the cause of Zion in his section to the state. His period of labor embraced the time of great conflict between Missionary Baptist and the Anti-Missionary Baptist, and fought for righteous cause of Missions in a truly soldier-like manner."

In August 1843, Elder James was chosen pastor of the New Hope Baptist Church, some twelve to fifteen miles east of Liberty. This church was organized in 1829, but had a rather checkered existence. First, the Anti-Missionary controversy diminishes its membership, so that when the minister began serving the church, it consisted of only twenty members. However, these members were staunch, and his labors with them were phenomenally successful for a county congregation. At times he would baptize as many as 60 converts at one time. Before he left to go to California his members had increased to two hundred.

During his stay in Missouri between 1847-1850 he established a number of churches in the thinly settled counties of Ray, Clay and Clinton where he was instrumental in organizing churches, some of which still exist and one particularly "Providence Baptist Church" is a model country church, up-to-date in method and spirit. Preaching was not the only passion for Robert James; he was also interested in education. A history of William Jewel College compiled by James G. Clark states that when the charter for the school was granted on February 27, 1849, Robert was one of twenty-six men appointed to be on the first Board of Trustees. Robert was a man of importance to the State of Missouri. Many of his churches that exist today became monuments to the man who rode horseback, carrying a Bible, in the dense woods of the frontier lands. His monuments are as real, but lesser known than those built by his horse riding and pistol carrying, so called outlaw-murdering sons, Frank and Jesse James.

Mr. Sames next goes into the family of Frank and Jesse James' mother as he states:

The background of Zerelda Cole is just as impressive. She was born January 29, 1825 in Woodford County Kentucky at her grandfather's (Richard Cole Jr.) **Black Horse Inn**. The brick portion was attached to the Inn in 1799. It was the living quarters of her father James Cole, born September 8, 1804 to February 27, 1827 and her mother Sarah (Sallie) Lindsay (4-15-1803 to 10-12-1851). She was the daughter of Anthony and Alsey (Cole) Lindsay. Alsey was the daughter of Richard Cole Sr. being James Cole's Aunt. After her husband Richard died in 1850, she was married to a Mr. Sims, who died. She married again to Mr. Samuels and had four more children, who were half brothers to Jesse and Frank James.

The Cole family had come from Pennsylvania through Virginia to Kentucky. Richard Cole Sr. helped to survey with Humphrey Marshall "The Vacant Lands", where Frankfort is now located in June and July of 1785. He later settled in Woodford County near what is now the town of Midway and Leestown Pike. He bought a large track of land from Hancock Lee. Hancock's son, Maj. John Lee helped in the settlement of Versailles, KY. Richard Cole Sr. operated a Tavern by the name, "**Cole's Inn**," located on Cole's Road, (later renamed Leestown Road.)

Mary J. Holmes wrote many books about this area and time, as this community was known by the notorious name of "*Little Sodom*" by many righteous people. The Inn, often called "**Cole's Bad Inn**," burned in the winter of 1811. The following year Richard's son Richard Cole Jr. bought out his father's former competitor on Old Frankfort Pike, **The Kennedy and Dailey Stagecoach Stopover**, and named his new business the **"Black Horse Inn."** The Inn was known far and wide and frequented by the likes of Henry Clay. The Tavern is still standing; a Gallery and Studio are operating a business there at present.

Richard Cole Jr. (4-23-1763 to 7-9-1839) married Sally Yates. He was a wealthy farmer; operated the **Black Horse Inn**; he was one of the first constables of Woodford County and was commissioned Lieutenant in the Woodford Light Infantry Company, November 10, 1796.

Most of the family is buried in the Cole Family Cemetery on a hilltop near the former Cole's Bad Inn. For more information see the Cole, James, and Graves Families.

There seems to be a striking similarity in the personalities of Richard and his granddaughter Zerelda, in their strong personalities, blunt acceptance of facts pleasant or unpleasant, high courage and almost fanatical loyalty to their families. They were friends to be desired and enemies to be feared and avoided. Richard Cole Junior's latter days were marred by violent and tragic events, which did not cease with his death but continued to plague his family unto "the third and forth generation."

Richard and Sallie's children were: William Cole, Mary Cole, Elizabeth Cole, Sally Cole, Jesse Cole, and Amos Cole who were killed in a fight at Black Horse Inn 1827. **(See the Frankfort Argus Newspaper dated May 27, 1827.**) James Cole (2-8-1804 to 9-27-1833) was married to his first cousin Sally Lindsay. She had only two children before his death. It is said he died after being thrown from a horse. Zerelda was then only two years old, she continued to live at the Black Horse Inn with her grandfather as guardian. After James' death her mother married again to Robert Thomason whom Zerelda did not favor. According to members of the family Zerelda "hated" Robert Thomason and became a favorite to her grandfather, Richard Cole Jr. who gave her the proper education and training to become a lady of prominence. When Sally and Robert moved to Clay County Mo., Zerelda did not accompany them, instead she went to live with her Uncle James M. Lindsay, at Stamping Ground, Scott Co. Ky. It was at the Church in Stamping Ground she and Robert James became engaged.

Mr. Sames next delves into the early life of Frank and Jesse James as he states:

Alexander Franklin James and Jesse Woodson James were born, respectively, on January 10, 1843 and September 5, 1847 on a farm near Kearney, Missouri, a town twelve miles northeast of the Clay County seat at Liberty and twenty-seven miles from downtown Kansas City to the Southwest. Robert Sallee James was a well-known ordained minister; their mother, Zerelda Cole, attended school at a Catholic convent in Lexington, KY. In 1842, shortly after being married, Robert and Zerelda left their native Kentucky to settle in Clay County, where Robert became pastor of a Baptist Church, acquired a farm and two slaves, and helped found William Jewell

College and Liberty, Missouri. Thus the family background of Frank and Jesse seems to have been quite solid and respectable.

But it did not remain so for long. In 1850, Robert joined the rush to California, some say in quest of gold. Others prefer to think he was ever the evangelist, and went to preach God's Word. The answer may be found in his last sermon at New Hope Baptist Church on the thirty first day of March 1850. He told his congregation that he was not interested in gold but rather in saving the souls of the gold miners. Instead he found illness and death. He died August 18, 1850 at Hang Town Gold Camp (later know as Placerville, El Dorado, CA). He was buried in an unmarked grave. His cause of death is not known, but there was a cholera outbreak in the area at the time. Zerelda remarried twice; first Benjamin Simms, who soon left her and then died.

In 1859, she married Doctor Reuben Samuel, a quiet, humble man who devoted himself to working the James' farm. Zerelda bore him four children: two boys and two girls. How young Frank and Jesse reacted to their father's departure and death, their mother's remarriages, and the influx of half brothers and sisters in unknown.

Mr. Sames next discusses the beginning of the Civil war and how the war affected Frank and Jesse James. A lot of this material is discussed from other sources later in this work but Mr. Sames gives details about some aspects that are not covered by them. These instances will be quoted:

Mr. Sames first tells of how Frank James first joined the pro-Confederate forces of Major General Sterling Price and took part in Battle of Wilson's Creek and the siege of Lexington, Missouri, September 12th through the 20th of 1861, but when Price retreated to Arkansas in 1862, Frank, as many other discouraged Rebels, deserted and returned home. He took an oath of allegiance to the United States and posted a $1,000 bond as good behavior.

Meanwhile, guerrilla war had broken out in Missouri. Bands of Kansas jayhawkers ravaged the western border, and Unionist militia prosecuted and plundered Confederate sympathizers.

By July 1862, bushwhacking was so rampant that the governor of Missouri ordered every man of military age to enroll in the state militia. Since this had the effect of forcing pro-Confederates to side with enemies against friends, many of them promptly "took to the bush." Among them was Frank James. In time he became a member of a Clay County guerrilla band headed by William "Bloody Bill" Anderson, a ferocious killer who decorated the bridle of his horse with the scalps of Federal soldiers. On August 21, 1863, Anderson and his gang, including Frank James, joined Quantrill in a raid on Lawrence, Kansas, where they helped massacre upward of 100 helpless men and boys. Other bloody and gruesome attacks soon followed which **Mr. Sames** details.

In the spring of 1864, the Anderson band returned to its "stomping ground" in Missouri. Soon after, Jesse James, now seventeen, joined the group which included his brother Frank. More than likely he would have done so in any case, at this point in time, Zerelda was married to Dr. Samuel and was pregnant. During the summer Union militia had harassed Mrs. Samuel, tortured Dr. Samuel, Frank and Jesse's stepfather, and administered a whipping to Jesse. This removed any hesitation he might have felt for taking up arms against the Union side. Under Anderson and riding behind Frank, he took part in numerous gruesome raids, robberies, ambushes, fights, and massacres.

Mr. Sames next describes the death of "Bloody Bill" Anderson. Militiamen subsequently killed Anderson in a fight outside Richmond Missouri, cut off his head, and mounted it to a telegraph pole.

At the same time the Federals routed Prices Army, which had invaded Missouri in a last desperate attempt to secure it for the Confederacy. Most of the bushwhackers, including Jesse, followed Price into Texas, where they spent the winter. However, Frank joined a number of guerrillas who went to Kentucky. Frank James along with Quantrill formed a new gang called Morgan's Raiders, with a new leader, Marcellus Jerome Clark (better known as Sue Mundy) and it totaled more than 50 guerrillas. On February 3, 1865, twenty-six guerrillas burned the town railroad depot at Midway, Kentucky. While the depot was burning, they robbed the stores and everybody they met, taking money, watches and jewelry and anything of value.

Sue Mundy was captured on March 11, 1865 in Mead County (Brandenburg, Ky). He was tried, found guilty and hanged in Louisville on Broadway near 18th Street on March 15, 1865.

Quantrill, along with Frank and 22-50 guerrillas continued to plunder throughout Kentucky towns and villages. At Brandenburg, during the early part of June 1866, Frank got into a fight with four Federal soldiers. The soldiers are said to have mistaken Frank for a horse thief and attempted to arrest him. Frank was wounded during the shoot-out, and wrote for Jesse to come to Brandenburg. Jesse did so, even though he was weak, and stayed until Frank had recovered, October 1866. Before Frank was wounded, he killed two, wounded a third, and was shot in the joint of the left hip by the fourth before he escaped.

Mr. Sames next goes into how Donny Pence and Frank James became lifelong friends as he states:

Captain Donnie Pence was in combat when he had his horse shot from under him and he was shot through the thigh. It was at this time that an incident occurred that forever made a friend of the notorious Frank James. "The Confederate" with the exception of Frank and Capt. Pence, had passed through a gate and before it could be closed, Pence, in order to cover the retreat of his comrades, turned his horse and single-handedly held at bay about 100 Federal Calvary.

At this time he had started to rejoin his men. The pursuing cavalry had closed in on him with a volley from their Carbines. Pence's horse was killed and he was wounded. The horse fell on top of Pence pinning him to the ground. Frank James seeing the condition of Pence, and realizing his danger, rode to the rescue. He succeeded in reaching Pence and rescuing him from the dangerous position, carrying him on his horse and out of danger. On account of this incident the warmest friendship began between Capt. Pence and Frank James.

Mr. Sames next discusses the death of Quantrill, and it is nothing like what can be seen in old movies, as he states:

Quantrill spent some time with a man named Dawson. Dawson's daughter, Nanny, asked Quantrill for his autograph and instead he wrote her a poem. One of the lines in his poem was "***though dark clouds are above me.***" Quantrill was right dark clouds were above him and the Confederacy. On May 10, 1865, he and his men were ambushed in a muddy Spencer County, KY barnyard. Quantrill had a new horse, one that was not used to sounds of battle. It reared and bucked in terror and before he could pull himself into the saddle, a heavy carbide slug smashed into his back,

13

spinning him into the barnyard. Federal Troops found him paralyzed from the shoulders down. Quantrill told them his name was Capt. William Clarke, of the Fourth Missouri Cavalry. He bribed Edward Terrill, the Federal officer in charge, saying he was in much pain, and asked the officer to let him stay in a nearby farmhouse, owned by James H. Wakefield.

Later that night Frank James and other survivors of Quantrill's last fight crawled out of the woods and came to Wakefield's house. They wanted to rescue Quantrill, but he told them he had promised Terrill he would not leave and that if he did, Yankee's would burn Wakefield's home in reprisal. Two days later the Federal Troops returned. By then they had learned that their famous prisoner was William Clarke Quantrill, famous guerrilla commander, and not some unknown Missouri cavalry captain. They loaded him into a wagon and hauled him to a hospital in Louisville, where he died on June 6, 1865, at the young age of twenty-seven.

Ironically, General Robert E. Lee had signed the Confederacy surrender papers, on Easter Sunday, more than a month before Quantrill was shot. But news traveled slowly, and the status of surrendering guerrillas was vague. Frank James and the rest of Quantrill's veterans, Donnie Pence, Bud Greggs, James Wilkerson, Joab Perry, Bud Pence, George Shepard, Oliver Shepard and Cole Younger, to mention a few, surrendered at Samuel's Depot, KY on July 26, 1865 and were paroled on orders by General John M. Palmer.

When the Quantrill guerrillas with Frank James first came to Kentucky, they went straight to the home of T.W. Samuels, cousin to Dr. Samuels who was Frank's stepfather. The reason given was that during the later days of the war, Quantrill's guerrillas were having a tough time finding a hideout and lacked provisions. Also, by coming to Kentucky, they could remain active in their rebel activities while having the security of being a part of the law, so to speak.

Old T.W. Samuels was elected High Sheriff of **Nelson County** in 1864, and in those days the Sheriff was local law. Much of Quantrill's army stayed at Samuels Depot. Two brothers, Donnie and Bud Pence, who rode with Quantrill for a period of two years were members of the first James Gang. Both eventually married Samuel's sisters and they both ended up in law enforcement.

Mr. Sames next discusses how Jesse James was shot trying to surrender as he states:

Jesse James was almost captured, on April 23, 1865. There seems to be quite a bit of confusion about what happened that morning. A.L. Maxwell of Lexington, MO, whose brother-in-law obtained the facts firsthand from Barnett Lankford, who willingly took Jesse in that night, reports the events of that day as follows: A group of men on horseback (guerrillas) were headed for Burns Schoolhouse where they intended to surrender. In this group was Jesse Hamlett, a friend of the family. They suddenly saw a band of five horsemen coming from the direction of Salt Pond Road. These men charged the guerrillas, firing on them.

Hamlett's horse was shot out from under him and Jesse James was shot three times, twice in the right breast and once in the leg. In spite of these wounds, Jesse got his friend up behind him and they rode as fast as they could. What happened to Hamlett is not known, but Jesse was so seriously injured that he had to dismount and crawl off the roadside into the brush. He then crawled into an old abandoned coal mine. When night came, he went up to a house, which proved to be the home of Barnett Lankford. He was a Southern sympathizer and willingly took Jesse into his home. Jesse stayed there for two days. By this time, he could stay on a horse; and painful though it was, he rode until he came to the Hill Farm where Dr. A. B. Hereford treated his wounds, Jesse returned the horse he had borrowed from Mr. Lankford by way of a veteran of Price's army, who had come to the Hill Farm with Jesse.

On this farm was an abandoned log house and in it Jesse hid until he was able to travel to his mother's home. She had been banished from her Missouri home to Rulla, Nebraska. In another story, Jesse was wounded; a bullet penetrated a short distance from the scar of the wound of August 1864. A bit of cloth may have been the thing that saved Jesse's life this time. He was wearing a flannel shirt and the bullet carried a piece of this cloth into the wound, and apparently helped stop the flow of blood from the wound. The existence of the cloth in the wound was not known at the time but months later he coughed up small recognizable bits of the flannel.

Mr. Simms now describes how Jesse James met and married Zee as he further states:

Jesse finally told his mother, Zerelda, that if he died, he did not want to die in the North. He asked to be taken back home. Dr. Samuels closed out his practice and they started their trip home in August of 1865. On the way back, they stopped at Aunt Mary Mimms, his father's sister, who lived in Kansas City. Here Jesse met

Zerelda Mimms, who nursed him while he was recovering from his wounds. As soon as he began to get better, they started again for home. During the return trip, Jesse told his mother that he wanted to marry his cousin, Zee (Zerelda Mimms) as he called her. It was not until April 4, 1874 that they got married.

Mr. Sames next describes just how the James Gang entered into a life of crime after the Civil War as he states:

It was thought that the war being over, and Jesse and Frank having been wounded, that the majority of the bushwhackers who wanted to settle down and lead a peaceful, law-abiding life would be able to do so. The trouble was that some of them did not want to, or at least did not try very hard. This was especially true of those whose criminal tendencies had been developed and confirmed by bushwhacking. Finding humdrum, poverty-tinged existence on a farm tedious after the exciting life and easy money of wartime, they could not resist the temptation to make use of the skills acquired under Quantrill and Anderson. A month later Jesse was in Clay Co., Mo.

On the afternoon of February 13, 1866, a dozen former bushwhackers looted the Clay County Savings Bank in Liberty Mo. of nearly $60,000, in the process murdering a student from William Jewell, the college Frank and Jesse's father helped establish. It was the first daylight bank robbery in American history, not counting the plundering of two banks in St. Albans, Vermont in 1864 by Confederate raiders operating out of Canada. It also marked the beginning of a series of bank holdups by gangs of guerrillas: Lexington, Mo., October 30, 1866; Savannah, Missouri, March 2, 1867; Richmond, Mo., May 22, 1867.

Mr. Sames now discusses Jesse James' complications from his chest wound as he states:

In June 1867, Jesse was in Nashville, Tenn. under the care of Dr. Paul Eve. He told Jesse that his lung was too badly decayed for cure and that the best thing he could do was to go home and die among his own people. From Nashville Jesse went to Logan County, KY. Jesse and the boys decided to rob a bank in Russellville, KY on March 20, 1868. Jesse James had five of his guerrillas (supposedly Jim White, Cole Younger, John Jarrette, George and O. Shepard). Cole had previously visited the bank of Nimrod Long and Company posing as a cattle dealer. A few days later the bank was robbed, and the gang escaped with a sum reportedly as high as $9,000.

Long, who refused to obey the robbers' orders, suffered a scalp wound when a bullet grazed his head. There are different stories where the robbers came from. One place was thought to be **Nelson County**, where Donnie Pence lived, and another story was that they stayed with their Uncle George Hite in Adairville, KY.

Probably Frank and Jesse participated in all of these robberies, although at the time they occurred, neither the authorities nor the newspaper accused them of involvement. But then, on December 7, 1869 in Gallatin, MO, two men entered the Daviess County Saving Bank, where one of them cold-bloodedly shot the cashier, a former Union militia officer, through the head and heart. As they left the bank carrying several bags of hundreds of dollars, townsmen opened fire. The bandit who murdered the cashier was unable to mount his excited horse, whereupon he jumped up behind his companion and together they galloped out of town. Several citizens identified the abandoned horse as a mare belonging to Kentucky robbers. A posse pursued the bandits to the James-Samuel farm, only to see Frank and Jesse dash out of a barn on fresh horses and escape.

The James brothers denied responsibility of the Gallatin murder and robbery and even obtained affidavits (of dubious worth) from people in Clay County swearing to their innocence. However, they refused to submit to arrest and stand trial claiming (with good cause) that they would be lynched like several other former bushwhackers suspected of crimes. Hence, they became, if they were not already, professional outlaws.

Mr. Sames now discusses the Northfield, Minnesota bank robbery that was disastrous for the James-Younger Band as he states:

So far all the robberies perpetrated by the James and Youngers had taken place in regions they were familiar with and where friends or relatives could aid them in case they needed to escape the law. Then, late in the summer of 1876, following a July 7 train stickup at Rocky Cut near Otterville, MO, a member of the gang known as Bill Chadwell (real name William Stiles) persuaded the rest of the gang that his home state of Minnesota offered rich and easy pickings. As a consequence, on the morning of September 7 eight men, all dressed in long, linen dusters, rode into Northfield, Minnesota. They were Frank and Jesse James, Cole and Bob Younger, Chadwell and two ruffians called Clell Miller and Charlie Pitts.

Three of the men dismounted and entered the First National Bank. They ordered cashier Joseph Heywood to open the vault. He refused. One of the robbers, probably either Jesse or Frank, shot him. The teller, A.E. Bunker, ran out the back door, undeterred by a bullet in the shoulder. Meanwhile several townsmen, having perceived that a robbery was in progress, opened fire with rifles and shotguns on the mounted men outside the bank. Two of them, Chadwell and Miller tumbled dead from their horses. Bullets from the robbers' revolvers in turn killed the sheriff and a Swedish immigrant who understood neither English nor what was happening.

The outlaws inside the bank rushed out, remounted, and along with the others galloped away under a hail of bullets. Bob Younger's horse went down. Bob, whose right elbow had been shattered by a rifle bullet, was picked up by a companion, most likely Cole Younger, then continued to fight.

As hundreds of grim-faced posse men scoured western Minnesota, the unsuccessful raiders sought to make their way back to Missouri. But they were slowed down by their ignorance of the countryside, heavy rain, and above all by the badly wounded Bob Younger. According to some accounts, Frank and Jesse proposed abandoning him, or possibly killing him. Cole, however, refused to allow it. Eventually the James' went off alone and reached home safely.

The Younger's and Pitts were less lucky. On September 21, 1876 near Madelia, Minnesota a posse cornered them in a swamp. A short, one-sided gun battle ensued. Pitts was killed and the Youngers, literally riddled with bullets, surrendered. After recovering sufficiently they stood trial for murder and attempted robbery. They pleaded guilty and were sentenced to life imprisonment in the Minnesota State Penitentiary at Stillwater. For three years following the Northfield fiasco, Frank and Jesse lay low. Contrary to the billboards of certain present-day tourist traps, neither then, nor at any other time, did they hide out in caves. Instead they lived under assumed names with their wives and children in places like Nashville, St. Louis, and even Kansas City.

As Frank once remarked, "Most people look alike in the city." Given the primitive identification devices and the haphazard police communication in the era, it was not necessary for them to adopt disguises or take elaborate precautions. In fact, law enforcement agencies lacked **both photographs and detailed descriptions**. All they knew was that they were tall, lanky, and bearded, which was not much to go on.

Then, in spectacular style, the James boys, or at least Jesse, came out of retirement. First, on October 8, 1879, a gang led by Jesse ransacked a safe aboard a train at Glendale, Missouri. Next, on July 15, 1881, they held up a Rock Island train near Winston, MO, murdering the conductor and a passenger. And on the night of September 7, 1881 (fifth anniversary of the Northfield raid), the gang robbed both the safe and the passengers on a Chicago & Alton train at Blue Cut, east of Independence. The engineer of the train stated that the leader of the bandits, before riding off, shook hands with him and said, "You are a brave man…here is $2 for you to drink to the health of Jesse James tomorrow morning." In addition, a Jackson County farmer who had been arrested for participating in the Glendale affair testified in court that Jesse had recruited him and provided him with a revolver and shotgun. As a result, only fanatics like Edwards continued to call Frank and Jesse guiltless victims of persecution.

Mr. Sames also gives more insight into the surrender of Dick Liddil before the meeting of Governor Crittenden of Missouri with Bob Ford in a Kansas City hotel at midnight on January 13, 1882 where the pardon of Dick Liddil was arranged as well as Frank and Jesse James' death or capture was agreed upon as he states:

On December 4, 1881 Bob Ford and a veteran bandit named Dick Liddil killed Wood Hite, also an outlaw and Frank and Jesse's cousin, in a quarrel over a woman.

Fearful that Jesse would kill him in revenge, Liddil arranged to surrender to Sheriff James A. Timberlake of Clay County after first obtaining assurances of leniency from Crittenden if he helped apprehend Jesse. On learning of this, Bob Ford realized that Jesse surely would suspect him as a friend of Liddil. Hence, he too contacted Timberlake and Crittenden, with the result that he and his brother agreed to tip-off Timberlake as to the time and place of the gang's next operation. For his part, Crittenden promised the Fords immunity from punishment and a share of the reward money.

Mr. Sames next discusses the killing of Jesse James in more detail than other sources as he states:

Late in March 1882, the Fords went to the house in St. Joseph, MO., where Jesse, under the alias of Thomas Howard, had been living with his wife and two children since November. Together with Jesse they planned to rob the bank in nearby Platte City on April 4. However, on the morning of April 3, while eating breakfast with the Fords, Jesse read in the Kansas City Times that Liddil had surrendered to the authorities. Immediately Bob Ford sensed that Jesse now knew that the Fords intended to betray him. So when Jesse removed his pistol belt, something he had never done before, and stood on a chair to dust a picture on the wall, Bob Ford possibly thought these two things. First, "that Jesse was seeking to throw me off guard by pretending to have confidence in me as a companion; second, that now or never is my chance. If I don't get him now he'll get me tonight." So he slowly pulled his revolver and fired. The bullet tore through the back of Jesse's skull behind the right ear, and "he fell like a log, dead."

Bob Ford was brought to trial in St. Joseph on a charge of murder. Charles and Bob pleaded guilty, were sentenced to death, and were **promptly pardoned by Crittenden**. Ten years later, in Creede, Colorado, Bob Ford himself fell victim to a murder's pistol, having achieved the gloomy notoriety of being "that dirty little coward that shot Mr. Howard." Charles Ford committed suicide in 1896.

By 1882 Frank James was thirty-nine and at least semi-retired from banditry. The murder of Jesse convinced him that if he was going to reach forty, he had better make peace with the law. Therefore, with Edwards serving as his intermediary, he surrendered to Crittenden at Jefferson City on October 5, 1882. Frank James faced trial twice, once at Gallatin, MO and again at Muscle Shoals, Alabama. Frank stood trial for his alleged crimes, and each time a sympathetic jury acquitted him for lack of convincing evidence. **It never was proven in a strictly legal sense that the James boys ever committed so much as a single robbery!**

During the years that followed his second acquittal, Frank managed to make just enough money working as a shoe clerk to get by on. Then he tried working as a theater guard, in St. Louis, and as a horse race starter at county fairs.

Mr. Sames discusses lastly his take on the James Brothers as he states:

If anything we should dispel some of the myths about the James. First, legend has it that the two brothers were brutal murders and came from an illiterate family. **First of all, the James' were never convicted of any crime, nor have any letters, or personal statements been found to the contrary**. No one knows for sure if any published story was accurate. Second, "The James brothers robbed banks and stole from the railroads because those two institutions were forcing people into poverty." They raised grain prices, forcing farmers to sell their farms. Jesse came to the aid of the downtrodden. As far as the James family being illiterate, that's completely false. There are many letters written both by Frank and Jesse and they were well thought out and well composed.

Mr. Sames ends "The Outlaws" with the best list of the outlaw events and robberies that I was able to uncover which will be include in its entirety:

A PARTIAL LIST OF OUTLAW EVENTS

8-7-1863	Frank James robbed David Mitchell-$1.25 & knife
8-21-1863	Frank & Jesse, Quantrill, Anderson killed 100 men
9-27-1864	Frank & Jesse gang killed 124 men Centralia, Ohio
10-1864	Bloody Bill Anderson Killed
2-3-1865	Morgan Raiders, Frank included burned Depot Midway
2-4-1865	Morgan Raiders, Stole Horses, killed Adam Harper
2-4-1865	Morgan Raiders, Stole Horses, Rob. Alexander Farm
3-10-1865	Jesse James got shot, got away
3-15-1865	Marcellus Clark (Sue Mundy) Hanged at Lou. KY
4-23-1865	Jesse James got shot, escaped
5-10-1865	Quantrill captured, shot in back, died 6-6-1865
7-29-1865	Frank James Paroled
2-13-1866	Liberty, MO Bank robbery
6-1866	Frank James shot in Brandenburg, KY
6-1867	Jesse James was reported living in Nashville
12-1867	They were in Chaplin, KY
3-20-1868	Russellville, KY robbed Nimrod Long & Co. Bank of $8,000 to $14,000
12-7-1869	Gallatin, MO Daviess Co. Saving Bank $700-$3,000
7-3-1871	Coryden, Iowa Osobock Bros.
4-29-1872	Columbia, KY Deposit Bank $200-$1,500
9-26-1872	The Box Office of the World Agriculture Exposition in Kansas City, $10,000
5-27-1873	St. Genevieve, MO $3,000-$4,000-$6,000
7-21-1873	Council Bluffs, Iowa Train Robbery Adair to Rock Island train, $3,000

1-15-1874	Arie Stage Coach Milburn to Hot Springs, watch, diamond stick pin, $4,000
1-31-1874	Grads Hill, MO train robbery, $10,000
4-7-1874	Austin Stagecoach, $3,000
4-24-1874	Jesse James married Zee Mims
8-30-1874	Lexington, MO, stagecoach robbery
1-27-1875	Archie Samuel, Jesse's half brother killed by Pinkerton
8-31-1875	Jesse James son born, Jesse Edward James
9-1-1875	Huntington, WV Bank $4,500-$10,000
12-1-1875	Muncie, Kansas, Kansas Pacific train $55,000
7-7-1876	Otterville-Rocky Cut, MO $15,000
9-7-1876	Northfield, Minn. 1st National Bank
12-7-1876	Tishomingo Savings Bank Corinth Mo.-MI $5,000
12-8-1876	Muncie, Kas. Kansas Pacific RR
10-8-1879	Glendale Train & Chicago Alton Train
9-8-1880	Mammoth Cave, Key Stagecoach robbery, watch, diamond ring, etc. +
3-11-1881	Muscle Shoals, Al. Gov. Pay Mast. $5,200
7-15-1881	Winston, MO Chicago-Rock Island & Pacific train
9-7-1881	Rocky Cut. MO Chicago-Alton Train $15,000

Banks robbed in similar fashion, not thought to be by Frank & Jesse James gang.

9-2-1867	Savannah, MO
5-22-1867	Richmond, MO
7-11-1881	Davis Sexton Bank, Riverton, Iowa

Chapter 3

Frank and Jesse James Pedigree.

Familysearch.org and One World Tree on Ancestry.com were used to construct this pedigree.

John James
    B. 1665 in Riddilyn, South Wales, Pembrokeshire, Wales.
    D. 1749 in New Britain, Bucks, Pennsylvania.

Married

1. **Elizabeth Evans**
    B. 1680 in Lianrhystud, Cardiganshire, Wales.
    D. 1749 in Montgomery, Pennsylvania.

Children

  *Thomas James born 1690 in Riddily South Wales, Pembrokeshire, Wales.
  *William James born 1692 in South, Pembrokeshire, Wales.
  *Sarah James born 9 May 1692 in Riddily, Pembrokeshire South, Wales.
  *Josiah James born about 1694 in Rhydwilym, Pembrokeshire South, Wales.
  *Isaac James born 1700 in Rhydwilym Chapel, Llandysilio, Carmarthenshire, Wales.

2. **Elizabeth Davis** married John James1689 in Wales.
    B. 1669 in Riddilyn, South Wales, Pembrokeshire, Wales.
    D. About 1749 in in New Britain, Bucks, Pennsylvania.

Children

  Rebecca James born about 1689 in Pembrokeshire, Wales.
  Joseph James born 1689 in Wales.
  Aaron James born 1689.

*Thomas James born 1690 in Riddily South Wales, Pembrokeshire, Wales.
William James born 1692 South Pembrokeshire, Wales.
*Sarah James born 9 May 1692 in Riddilyn, Pembrokeshire South, Wales.
*Josiah James born 1694 in Rhydwilym, Pembrokeshire South,Wales.
*Isaac James born 1700 in Rhydwilym Chapel, Llandysilio, Carmarthenshire, Wales.

* Listed twice.

William James
B. Born 1692 in South Pembrokeshire, Wales.
D. 1778 in in New Britain, Bucks, Pennsylvania.

Married

Mary Hines born about 1694 in Pembrokeshire, England.
D. 1778 in Bucks, Pennsylvania.

Children

John James born 1719 in Bucks, Pennsylvania.
Margaret James born about 1726 in New Britain, Bucks, Pennsylvania.
Isaac James born about 1726 in New Britain, Bucks, Pennsylvania.
Abel James born 1729 in New Britain, Bucks, Pennsylvania.
Rebecca James born about 1730 in New Britain, Bucks, Pennsylvania.

John James
B. 1719 Bucks, Pennsylvania.
D. 1785 New Britain, Bucks, Pennsylvania.

Married

Elizabeth Evans
B. 1720 in Pennsylvania.

Children

Josiah James born 1741 in New Britain, Bucks, Pennsylvania.
Isaac James born 1744 in New Britain, Bucks, Pennsylvania.
Ebenezer James born 1746 in New Britain, Bucks, Pennsylvania.
Simon James born 1748 in New Britain, Bucks, Pennsylvania.
Morgan James born 27 April 1752 in New Britain, Bucks, Pennsylvania.
William James born 1754 in Kings Stanley, Lasboro, Glouchestershire, England.
Elizabeth James born 1754 in New Britain, Bucks, Pennsylvania.
Mary James born 1756 in New Britain, Bucks, Pennsylvania.
Alice James born 1758 in New Britain, Bucks, Pennsylvania.

William James
B. 1754 in Kings Stanley, Lasboro, Glouchestershire, England.
D. 1805 in Lickinghole Creek, Goochland, Virginia.

Married

Mary Hines on July 15, 1754 in Hanover, Virginia.

Children

Samuel James 1774-1836
John M. James 1775-1827
Mary James 1776-
Nancy Ann James 1777-
William James 1782-1807
Thomas James 1783-
Martin James 1784-
Richard James 1785-

John M. James
B. 1775 in Hanover, Virginia.
D. 1827 in Logan, Kentucky.

Married

1. Mary G. Poor
  B. 1790 in Goochland, Virginia.
  D. February 1827 in Logan, Kentucky.

Children

*Mary James born September 28, 1809 in Goochland, Virginia. Married John Mimms. **Parents of Zerelda Mimms, wife of Jesse James.**
*John R. James Born February 15, 1815 in Logan, Kentucky.
*Nancy Gardner James born September 13, 1821 in Logan, Kentucky. Married George Hite. **Parents of Wood and Clarence Hite.**
*Thomas Martin James born April 8, 1823 in Logan, Kentucky.
*Drury Woodson James born November 14 in Logan, Kentucky.

2. Mary Polly Poor
  B. 1790 in Goochland, Virginia.
  D. February 1807 in Logan, Kentucky.

Children

*Mary James born September 28, 1809 in Goochland, Virginia.
  William James born September 11, 1811 in Logan, Kentucky.
*John R. James born February 15, 1815 in Logan, Kentucky.
Elizabeth James born November 25, 1816 in Logan, Kentucky. Married Tillman   West.
Robert Sallee James born July 7, 1818 in Logan, Kentucky.
*Nancy Gardner James born September 13, 1821 in Logan, Kentucky.
*Thomas Martin James born April 8, 1823 in Logan, Kentucky.
*Drury Woodson James born November 14, 1826 in Logan, Kentucky.
Mary Elizabeth James born 1827 in Logan County, KY. Married John R. (Hugh) Cohorn.

  *Listed twice.

Robert Sallee James

    B. July 17, 1818 in Logan, Kentucky.

    D. August 18, 1850 in Placerville, California.

Married

Zerelda Cole

    B. January 29, 1825 in Woodford, Kentucky.

    D. February 10, 1911 in Oklahoma City, Oklahoma.

Children

    Alexander Franklin James Born January 10 1843 in Kearney, Clay, Missouri.
    Robert R. James born July 19, 1845 in Kearney, Clay, Missouri.
    Jesse Woodson James born September 5, 1847 in Kearney, Clay, Missouri.
    Susan Lavenia James born November 25, 1849 in Kearney, Clay, Missouri.

I feel that this is the appropriate time to develop the family patriarchal pedigrees of Elvira James, Stephen H. Rogers and add information about William Joshua Rogers family.

Chapter 4

Elvira I. James Patriarchal Pedigree

From family stories, Elvira I. James was first cousin to Frank and Jesse James. This means that Elvira I. James' father, Joshua James was the son of one of John M. James' sons, or her mother Esther Hicks James was the sister of Zerelda Cole James.

There's one mention on One World Tree for the father of Joshua James 1 as being the son of Thomas M. James. This would have been the pedigree scenario of Elvira I. James if this were true.

John M. James
    B. 1775 in Hanover, Virginia.
    D. 1827 in Logan, Kentucky.

Married

1. **Mary G. Poor**
    B. 1790 in Goochland, Virginia.
    D. February 1827 in Logan, Kentucky.

Children

    *Mary James born September 28, 1809 in Goochland, Virginia. Married John Mimms. **Parents of Zerelda Mimms, wife of Jesse James.**
    *John R. James Born February 15, 1815 in Logan, Kentucky.
    *Nancy Gardner James born September 13, 1821 in Logan, Kentucky. Married George Hite. **Parents of Wood and Clarence Hite.**
    ***Thomas Martin James** born April 8, 1823 in Logan, Kentucky.
    *Drury Woodson James born November 14 in Logan, Kentucky.

2. **Mary Polly Poor**
    B. 1790 in Goochland, Virginia.
    D. February 1807 in Logan, Kentucky.

Children

    *Mary James born September 28, 1809 in Goochland, Virginia.
William James born September 11, 1811 in Logan, Kentucky.
*John R. James born February 15, 1815 in Logan, Kentucky.
Elizabeth James born November 25, 1816 in Logan, Kentucky. Married
Tillman West.
Robert Sallee James born July 7, 1818 in Logan, Kentucky.
*Nancy Gardner James born September 13, 1821 in Logan, Kentucky.
*Thomas Martin James born April 8, 1823 in Logan, Kentucky.
*Drury Woodson James born November 14, 1826 in Logan, Kentucky.
Mary Elizabeth James born 1827 in Logan County, KY. Married John R,
(Hugh) Cohorn.

    *Listed twice.

Thomas Martin James
    B. April 8, 1823 in Logan, Kentucky.

Children

From the 1850-1870 U.S Census information found on Ancestry.com.

Wife named **Sarah.**

    John W. Crawford James
    Luther James

Thomas Martin James was apparently a successful business leader in Kansas City,
Missouri and had two of his sons working with him in the endeavor.

Joshua James 1 - From One World Tree on Ancestry.com.
    B. About 1775
    D. About 1823 in Dickson, Tennessee.

His father was listed as Thomas James and his grandparents were listed as John James and Mary Francis.

Married

Abby. No other information is given.

Children - No birth dates given.

> James James
> William James
> Sally James
> **Joshua James 2**
> Amos James
> Thomas James
> Elijah James
> Abby James
> Enoch James Born 1795.

Joshua James 2
> B. About 1808 in Tennessee.
> **D. 1921 in Tennessee.**

Married

1. Nancy James
2. Nancy Powell B. About 1816 D.1899

Children

> Johnson M. James born December 14, 1832 in Hickman, Tennessee.
> Mary C. James born March 30, 1840 in Arkansas.

From the William Pierce Gray Phillips of Tennessee and Alabama family tree.

Joshua James 2 was the son of **Joshua James 1** but the search ended here even though both came from Tennessee, which is not too far from Logan County,

Kentucky where the ancestors of Frank and Jesse James lived at the time. The name of the wives of Joshua James 2 did not match the name of the wife of Joshua James 3, Esther Hicks, the supposed grandparents of William Joshua Rogers. They appear to be two distinct families.

> *It was mentioned for Joshua James 1 that his father was Thomas James (Thomas Martin James?). I was unable to find any mention on the internet of Thomas (Thomas Martin James) or any of his brothers having a son named Joshua James.*
>
> *I was also unable to tie in any relationship from information on the internet between the Cole Family and the Hicks family.*

The family stories are too strong and numerous to deny that such a relationship existed, only that there is not enough information on the internet to allow such a direct tie.

Joshua James 3
> B. 1807 in Tennessee.
> D. January 26, 1881 in Greenhill, Lauderdale County, Alabama.
> B. Hill cemetery near Greenhill in Lauderdale County, Alabama according to the Williams Pierce Gray Phillips of Tennessee and Alabama family tree.

I was unable to find the names of the parents of Joshua James 3. While Joshua James 3 was born in Tennessee, he spent most of his time in Lauderdale County, Alabama. While the internet is silent, Joshua James 3 could have been the son of Joshua James 1 and confused with Joshua James 2 on the internet at some point.

Another case of the silence of the endless and fathomless "Black Bog of Time" from which no accurate information will ever escape!

Married

Esther Hicks 1807 - 1881

Occupation and Residences of Joshua James from a summary of various U.S. Census records:

1850 - Occupation Blacksmith, with two students working with him.
1850 - Division 2 East of the Military Road, Lauderdale County, Alabama.
1870 - Township 1 Range 8, Lauderdale County, Alabama.
1880 - Lauderdale County, Alabama.
1881 - Death January 26, 1881 at age 74. Buried in the Hill Cemetery, Greenhill, Lauderdale County, Alabama according to the Williams, Pierce Gray Philips of Tennessee and Alabama family tree. Knox, Tennessee according to One World Tree.

Another interesting point, both Joshua and Esther died on January 26, 1881 according to internet sources. Was there a common cause such as a house fire or an epidemic of some sort? The dark and endless black bog of time is silent.

Children

> Sarah C. James 1830-
> Harriet S. James 1832-1853
> Mary H. James 1836-1858
> **Elvira I. James** 1837-1861
> Isabella James 1838-
> Richard James 1842-
> Joshua James 1845-
> California James 1847-

1850 US Census
The family's residences were as listed above. People living with Joshua James and Esther Hicks James are listed as follows:

Joshua James	43
Esther James	43
Sarah James	18
Harriet James	17
Mary James	16
Elvira James	**15**
Isabella James	12

Richard James	8
Joshua James	5
California James	3
Holden Simmons	21
Samuel Ransey	30

1870 U.S. Census

Joshua James	62
Esther James	61
Sallie James	38
Joshua James	23
Isabella Matthews	26
Marion Matthews	7
William Rogers	8
R. M. Hicks	75

1880 U. S. Census

| Joshua James | 72 |

His father and mother's birthplace was stated to be Maryland. This is of special interest later. It was stated on a typed copy of the census that I have that their birthplace was MA which is now the common abbreviation for Massachusetts.

Esther James	72
Isabella James	40
William Matthews	18
William Rogers	19
Esther Bell	9
Dwight Bell	7
Emma Bell	4

Joshua James 3 died in 1881 and is reportedly buried in the Hill cemetery near Greenhill, Lauderdale County, Alabama by the Williams, Pierce Gray Phillips of Tennessee and Alabama family tree.

Chapter 5

Stephen H. Rogers Patriarchal Pedigree

Joseph Rogers, Sr.
   B. 1748

Joseph Rogers Jr.
   B. About 1776
   M. 13 October 1797 in Granville County, N.C.
   D. In Greenville County N.C.

Married

   Dora Dicey Kittrell born 1776 died 1851 on 14 October 1797 in Granville County, N.C.

Children
   Sarah Leah Rogers born 1798.
   Samuel Rogers born 1799 in Granville County, N.C.
   John Rogers born about 1800 in Granville County, N.C.
   Jonathan T. Rogers born about 1801 in Granville County, N.C.
   Martha Rogers born 1803.
   Rachael Rogers born about 1805 in Granville County, N.C.
   Mary Nancy Rogers born about 1813 in Granville County, N.C. died 1838.
   Willis Rogers born about 1819 in Granville County, N.C.

Samuel Rogers
   B. 1799 in Granville County, N.C.
   M. 4 January 1829 in Morgan County, Alabama.
   D. Lauderdale County, Alabama.

Married

   Mary White B. 1800

Children

Stephen H. Rogers
B. 1832 in Rogersville, Lauderdale County, Alabama.
D. 1864 at Elmira, New York in a Prisoner of War (POW) prison.

Stephen H. Rogers was listed on Ancestry.com as being in the Confederate Army. He enlisted as a private in Company H of the 57th regiment of the Alabama Infantry.

He died October 17, 1864 and is buried in the Woodlawn National Cemetery, Elmira, New York as a prisoner of war.

Cemeteries - Woodlawn National Cemetery

Woodlawn National Cemetery
1825 Davis Street
Elmira, NY 14901
Phone: (607) 732-5411
FAX: (607) 732-1769

Office Hours:
Monday thru Friday - 8:00 a.m. to 4:00 p.m.
Closed federal holidays.

Visitation Hours:
Open daily from sunrise to sunset.

Burial Space: This cemetery has space available for cremated remains in a columbarium. We can accommodate casketed remains of subsequent family members in the same gravesite of previously interred family members.

Acreage: 10.5

Number of Interments
Thru Fiscal Year 2008: 9,087

General Information Kiosk on Site? No

Floral/Ground Regulations

Directions from nearest airport:
Cemetery is located in Chemung County, Elmira, N.Y., next to Woodlawn City Cemetery. Take Interstate 86 to Exit 52B, Route 14 South, Elmira Heights. Follow Route 14 South for approximately two miles until you come to a Y in the road. Bear right at the Y. Follow Oakwood Avenue. After one mile Oakwood Avenue will change to Davis Street. Follow Davis Street. The cemetery will be on your right.

General Information   Historical Information   Notable Persons

GENERAL INFORMATION

A gravesite locator is located to the right of the office door.

Military Funeral Honors
The cemetery staff can assist funeral homes by providing the telephone numbers for the Military Funeral Honors contacts.

Military Funeral Honors are organized under the Department of Defense and should be arranged by the funeral director. In the event there is not a funeral director involved in making arrangements please refer to the telephone numbers listed below or contact your local American Legion or VFW.

Army and National Guard - (607) 664-4909
Navy and Merchant Marine - (860) 694-3475
Air Force - (716) 236-3182 or (518) 344-2586
Marine Corps - (516) 228-5666
Coast Guard - (216) 902-6117
back to top

HISTORICAL INFORMATION

Woodlawn National Cemetery is located in Elmira, N.Y., in Chemung County. In 1861, the town was both a training and marshalling center for Union soldiers during the Civil War. As trainees were eventually assigned to military units and the barracks emptied, the federal government used the buildings as a prisoner-of-war camp. Originally known as Camp Rathbun, and designated Camp No. 3 during its existence from summer 1864 until the end of the war, this camp housed approximately 12,000 Confederate enlisted men. Approximately 3,000 men died here.

Confederate POWs were transported by rail from locations such as Point Lookout, Md., and Old Capital Prison in Washington, D.C., to Elmira. Upon arrival, most of the captives were in poor physical condition, which was only exacerbated by their incarceration. While the weather was mild during summer and fall, in its first year approximately 900 prisoners were without housing until early January. Prison records show that men died from typhoid fever, dysentery and pneumonia, as well as malnutrition. The Confederates lacked adequate rations and medical care thanks to insufficient medical supplies. Prisoners infected with smallpox were often moved to a remote location and forgotten. It was not uncommon to see a frozen body lying outside a tent waiting to be loaded for transportation to the cemetery. Another contributing factor to the problem of disease was a stagnant pool known as Foster's Pond. This pond stood between the camp and the river.

Each day, deceased soldiers were placed in coffins and loaded on a buckboard wagon, up to nine at a time. The wagons traveled approximately a mile and a half to the cemetery, where a long trench was dug and the coffins placed in it side by side. At the time of the Confederate burials, John Jones, an escaped slave who found freedom in Elmira, was the sexton of Woodlawn Cemetery. He kept a meticulous record of each Confederate burial so that when, in 1907, the federal government was authorized to erect a small marble headstone at each grave, it was possible to inscribe them with the soldier's name, company regiment and grave number.

Beginning in February 1865, prisoners who swore allegiance to the Union were deemed eligible for release. Groups of approximately 500 men were allocated food rations, money and/or transportation vouchers and placed on a train bound for the major Union army supply depot in City Point, Va., where arrangements were made for the final trip home.

Soldiers who survived were released in groups at the end of the war and provided the same assistance. Approximately 140 went to the regional army hospital in Elmira where they were treated until fit to travel. Seventeen of them never recovered and died in New York. By the end of 1865, the camp was fully closed and all buildings razed or moved to nearby locations.

Woodlawn National Cemetery was listed on the National Register of Historic Places on Oct. 6, 2004.

Monuments and Memorials
The United States government erected the Shohola Monument in 1911 to commemorate a tragic railroad accident that took the lives of both Confederate and Union soldiers during the Civil War. Starting in 1906, the government began a program to mark the graves of Confederate prisoners

of war and this monument was one of the earliest monuments to be erected. One side of the Shohola monument honors 49 Confederate prisoners of war who were killed in the accident. According to 1864 newspaper accounts of the accident, the Confederate soldiers killed were among 853 Confederate prisoners being transported by train from the prison camp at Point Lookout, Maryland, to Elmira, New York, in July 1864. The 18-car passenger train which carried the prisoners of war was hit by a 50-car coal train on July 15, 1864. A total of 64 Confederate and Union soldiers were killed, along with the passenger train's engineer, 2 firemen, and a brakeman. One hundred and twenty other passengers were wounded. The other side of the Shohola monument commemorates the 17 Union guard sentinels - all privates of the 11th Veteran Reserve Corps - who accompanied the prisoners enroute to Elmira. Original burial location for the dead was in a trench near the accident site. They were later reinterred at Woodlawn National Cemetery and their individual remains were unidentifiable.

In 1937, the United Daughters of the Confederacy erected a monument in memory of those Confederate prisoners of war who died while imprisoned at Elmira and who are buried at Woodlawn National Cemetery. The bronze figure and granite monument overlooks the entire length of the Confederate area, facing eastward.

On Aug. 13, 1988, the Chemung County Veterans dedicated a monument in memory of all veterans from New York and Pennsylvania. The granite and bronze plaque memorial features military insignia from all five branches of the military.

NOTABLE PERSONS

back to top

FLORAL/GROUNDS REGULATIONS

Cemetery policies are conspicuously posted and readily visible to the public.

Floral arrangements accompanying the casket or urn at the time of burial will be placed on the completed grave. Natural cut flowers may be placed on graves at any time of the year. They will be removed when they become unsightly or when it becomes necessary to facilitate cemetery operations such as mowing.

Artificial flowers and potted plants will be permitted on graves during periods when their presence will not interfere with grounds maintenance. As a general rule, artificial flowers will be allowed on graves from Oct. 15 to April 15. Artificial flowers and potted plants may be placed on graves for a period extending 10 days before through 10 days after Easter Sunday and Memorial Day.

Christmas wreaths, grave blankets and other seasonal adornments may be placed on graves from Dec. 1 through Jan. 20. They may not be secured to headstones or markers.

Permanent plantings, statues, vigil lights, breakable objects and similar items are not permitted on the graves. The Department of Veterans Affairs does not permit adornments that are considered offensive, inconsistent with the dignity of the cemetery or considered hazardous to cemetery personnel. For example, items incorporating beads or wires may become entangled in mowers or other equipment and cause injury.

Permanent items removed from graves will be placed in an inconspicuous holding area for two weeks prior to disposal. Decorative items removed from graves remain the property of the donor but are under the custodianship of the cemetery. If not retrieved by the donor, they are then governed by the rules for disposal of federal property.
back to top

Stephen H. Rogers
>   B. 1832 in Rogersville, Lauderdale County, Alabama.
>   D. 1864 at Elmira, New York.

Married

Elvira I. James 1837-1861

Children

William Joshua Rogers.
>   B. December 1860 in Rogersville, Lauderdale County, Alabama.
>   D. 1948 in Lauderdale County, Alabama.

William Joshua Rogers owned a general country mercantile store near or in Altas. His daughter, Ona Rogers, ran the store in later years.

Married

Matilda W. M. Hill 1862-1954 in 1888 in Lauderdale County Alabama.

Children

>   Ella Rogers 1889-1988
>   Ona Rogers 1889-1981
>   Sallie Rebecca Rogers 1891-1914
>   Leona Rogers 1893-1981
>   Ira Norman Rogers 1898-1969
>   Mayme Esther Rogers 1900-1977. Married Gus Gray and is Finney Gray's mother along with several other children.
>   William Kilsey Rogers 1904-1974
>   Clara Rogers 1907-2009

There is not much information on the internet for William Joshua and Matilda Rogers' children listed immediately above.

Chapter 6

William Joshua Rogers Family

Scenario I

Rogers, Hicks and James Families

In this scenario the family comes from North Carolina

Raleigh Hicks
> B 1737 NC
> M 1755 NC

Mrs. Raleigh Hicks
> B 1737 NC
> M 1755 NC

Children

James Hyson Hicks
> B 1758 Virginia
> **M 1** Married **Mary Elizabeth Rogers** born 1768 in Virginia in 1796 Boston, Suffolk, MA.
> **M 2** Married **Rebecca Knight.** No information could be located about Rebecca. She is reported to be the mother of Rebecca Hicks born 1798 in Edgecombe, NC.
> **M 3** Married **Mary Rodgers.** No information could be located about Mary. She is reported to be the mother of Richard N. Hicks born 1794 in Knox, TN.
> **M 4** he married **Polley Rogers** born about 1772 in Person County NC.
> D 1850 Limestone, AL

Children

Isaac Hicks born 1790 in Edgecombe, NC.

Henry Hicks born 1792 in Edgecombe, NC.
Richard N. Hicks born 1794 in Knox, TN.
Rebecca Hicks born 1798 in Edgecombe, NC.
Hinson Rogers Hicks born 1 January 1801.
Esther Hicks born December 1807 in Edgecombe, NC.
? Hicks born 1809 in Edgecombe, NC.
Polly Hicks born 1811 in Edgecombe, NC.

Esther Hicks

B. December 1807, Edgecombe, NC
M. 1824 Edgecombe, NC
Died. July 1881 Knox, TN by One World Tree.
Buried July 1881 Knox, TN by One World Tree. In the Hill Cemetery near Greenhill, Alabama by the Williams Pierce Gray Phillips of Tennessee and Alabama family tree.

Married

Joshua James

B 1805 Knox, TN by one account, simply Tennessee by another.
M 1824 Edgecombe, NC

Children

Sarah James born about 1832.
Harriet James born about 1833 in Alabama.
Mary James born about 1834 in Alabama.
Elvira I. James born about1835 in Alabama.
Isabella James born about 1838 in Alabama.
Richard James born about 1842 in Alabama.
Joshua L. James born about 1845 in Alabama.
California James born about 1848 in Alabama.

Elvira I. James

B. 1837 in Lauderdale County, Alabama.
D. 04 August 1861 in Rogersville, Lauderdale County, Alabama.
Buried Liberty Cemetery near Rogersville, Alabama.

Married

Stephen H. Rogers.
 B. 1832 in Lauderdale County, Alabama.
 D. 17 October 1864 in Woodlawn National Cemetery, 1825 Davis Street, Elmira, New York 14901.

Children

William Joshua Rogers
 B. 1860
 D. 1948.

Rogers Family

Joseph Rogers, Sr.
 B. 1748

Joseph Rogers Jr.
 B. About 1776
 M. 13 October 1797 in Granville County, N.C.
 D. In Greenville County N.C.

Married

 Dora Dicey Kittrell born 1776 died 1851on 14 October 1797 in Granville County, N.C.

Children

 Sarah Leah Rogers born 1798.
 Samuel Rogers born 1799 in Granville County, N.C.
 John Rogers born about 1800 in Granville County, N.C.
 Jonathan T. Rogers born about 1801 in Granville County, N.C.
 Martha Rogers born 1803.
 Rachael Rogers born about 1805 in Granville County, N.C.

Mary Nancy Rogers born about 1813 in Granville County, N.C. died 1838.
Willis Rogers born about 1819 in Granville County, N.C.

Samuel Rogers
B. 1799 in Granville County, N.C.
M. 4 January 1829 in Morgan County, Alabama.
D. Lauderdale County, Alabama.

Married

Mary White
B. 1800

Children

Stephen H. Rogers
B. 1832.
D. 1864

Married

Elvira I. James
B. 1837 in Lauderdale County, Alabama.
D. 04 August 1861 in Rogersville, Lauderdale County, Alabama.
Buried Liberty Cemetery near Rogersville, Alabama.

Children

William Joshua Rogers
B. 1860
D. 1948

Chapter 7

Scenario II

Robert Rogers Family

In this scenario the family comes from South Carolina.

This scenario assumes that William Joshua Rogers was fathered by Coleman Rogers, one of Robert Rogers' sons and was taken mostly from the family tree "Lamberts and Dozens of Cousins" by Ruby Lambert on Ancestry.com.

Robert Rogers

    Born 1773 in South Carolina
    Died 1850 in Tuscaloosa County, Alabama

Married 1793 in South Carolina **Catherine ?** Born 1775.

1850 residence was District 2, Tuscaloosa, Alabama.

Children

    Minnie Rogers
    Nancy Rogers 1796 - 1890.
    William Rogers 1796 - 1880.
    Richard Rogers 1797 - 1884.
    Thomas Rogers 1800 -
    Richard Hampton Rogers 1806 - 1876.
    John Rogers 1814 -
    Coleman Rogers 1815 - 1880.

Coleman Rogers

    B. 1815 in Tennessee.
    D. 1880 in **Giles County, Tennessee.**

Marriage 1. March 1840 **Mary Caroline Lee** born 1823.

Children

> Caroline Elizabeth Rogers born 1840.
> John Thomas Rogers born 1843.
> Mary D. Rogers born 1844.
> Lucinda S. Rogers born 1845.
> Malcolm Coleman "Tobe" Rogers 1846 - 1925.
> James H. Rogers born 1847.
> Wiley Richard Rogers 1849 - 1931.
> Nancy A. Rogers 1849 - 1940.
> Francis Marion "Jack" Rogers born 1854.
> Melvina Rogers 1855 - 1933.
> Robert W. Rogers born 1857.

M2. **Lydia Polly** 1820 - 1868

> **William Joshua Rogers 1860 - 1948.**
> Isaac Rogers born 1863.

M3. **Lematine Rogers** spouse born 1846.

> Benjamin Rogers born 1871.
> Edward Rogers born 1872.
> Della Rogers born 1873.
> Joseph Rogers born 1874.

Seventeen children in all! This is quite an achievement if true. He would have been fathering children up until six years before he died in 1880 at the age of about 65!

Residences of William Joshua Rogers.
> B. 1860 in Rogersville, Alabama.
> Residence 1870 Township 15 Fayette, AL.
> Residence 1900 Precinct 5 Green Hill, Lauderdale County, Alabama.
> Residence 1910 Atlas, Lauderdale County, Alabama.
> Residence 1920 Atlas, Lauderdale County, Alabama.

Residence 1930 Atlas, Lauderdale County, Alabama.
D. 1948 Lauderdale County, Alabama.

Married

Matilda W. M. Hill 1862 - 1953.

Children

Ella Rogers born 1890.
Sallie Rogers born 1892.
Leona D. Rogers born 1895.
Ira Norman Rogers 1898 - 1969.
Mayme Rogers born 1901.
William Kelsie Rogers 1904 - 1974.
Clara Rogers born 1907.

<u>Scenario III</u>

In this scenario the family comes from South Carolina.

This scenario assumes that William Joshua Rogers was fathered by Richard Hampton Rogers, another son of Robert Rogers and it was developed from information found in the Lamberts and Dozens of Cousins, Clark-Marlow and Stearns family trees on Ancestry.com and offers a somewhat different take on Scenarios I and II.

The slightly different take on Scenario II is that William J. Rogers was born in Fayette, Alabama and his father was Richard Hampton Rogers, the son of Robert Rogers. His mother was Elizabeth Drake Rogers. A pedigree is as follows and plugs directly into the pedigree of Scenario II:

Robert Rogers
Born 1773 in South Carolina
D. 1850 in Tuscaloosa County, Alabama.

Married 1793 in South Carolina **Catherine ?** Born 1775.

1850 residence was District 2, Tuscaloosa, Alabama.

Children

Minnie Rogers
Nancy Rogers 1796 - 1890.
William Rogers 1796 - 1880.
Richard Rogers 1797 - 1884.
Thomas Rogers 1800 -
Richard Hampton Rogers 1806 - 1876.
John Rogers 1814 -
Coleman Rogers 1815 - 1880.

Richard Hampton Rogers
B. 1805 or 1806
D. 1876

Married

Elizabeth Drake Olive
B. 1811
D. 1886

Children–As listed on the 1870 US census from Fayette, Alabama.

Name	Age
John Rogers	29
Matilda Rogers	26
Mary Rogers	23
Catharine Rogers	18
Frances Rogers	17
Richard Rogers	16
Haywood Rogers	15
Lucy Rogers	12
Cate Rogers	11
William Rogers	**9**

William J. Rogers

     B. about 1861 in Fayette, Alabama.

I had to do further research at this point using One World Family Tree as well as the Hicks family tree on Ancestry.com to fully develop this scenario. It was found that this person was probably not William J. Rogers but William R. Rogers as documented from these family trees. The further development of this scenario was dropped at that point.

Chapter 8

Billy Rogers' Family Stories

Billy said that he spent a lot of time with his grandfather William Joshua Rogers while growing up. He said that he shaved William Joshua later in life and William Joshua died on Highway 43 a short distance from Billy's house while walking from his old log house to visit with Billy. William Joshua's old log house was near the intersection of current highway 43 and 64, or the Sam Davis Highway as it was known to me while growing up. Highway 64 connects Lexington, Alabama with Highway 43 just south of Greenhill. The recent Donnie's Market was near the site of William Joshua's old log house and general store. Billy's brother Tom built a house near William Joshua's old log house where he lived until his death in 2005.

Billy remembers the orchards and vineyards that William Joshua also had around his old log house and general store. There were bountiful fruits of all types each year: apples, peaches and grapes. Billy said that William Joshua didn't grow the fruit to sell. He shared it with family members and friends.

Billy recounted the following stories that William Joshua had told him at various times:

William Joshua Rogers came out of Giles County, Tennessee as a young man with L. D. Holloway and Morgan Matthews. All three of them were orphans with William Joshua Rogers' dad dying in a Civil War prisoner of war camp and his mother dying in Rogersville, Alabama shortly after his birth. Someone in Giles County, Tennessee took all three lads in for a time. All three of them opened retail store businesses in Lauderdale County, Alabama. Morgan Matthews owned a store in East Florence and continued to visit with William Joshua Rogers at William Joshua's log house. Billy remembers Morgan Matthews' visits when he was a young boy. L. D. Holloway became quite prosperous as the owner of Holloway Town on Brush Creek and as an official in the Woodmen of the World Insurance Company. Ona Rogers, a daughter of William Joshua, operated his general store after William Joshua's death. The author remembers buying things from Ona as a young boy growing up.

William Joshua told of it snowing one night after he went to bed as a young man. Snow was covering the bed covers when he woke up. The wind had blown the snow through the cracks in the walls of the log house. Billy didn't remember if this happened in Giles County, Tennessee or Lauderdale County, Alabama.

William Joshua told of going to Florence Alabama in a horse drawn wagon shortly after moving back to Lauderdale County. The wagon wheels started squeaking. Back then they used beef tallow to lubricate wagon wheels. William Joshua told of stopping at an old house back in a field near where Uncle Doc Tidwell finally built his house. A scraggly looking woman with unkempt hair came out of the house and they described their predicament to her and ask her if she had any tallow they could get. The old woman said "I don't have any tallow to grease my own gut, let alone to fix your dammed old wagon!" Billy says that William Joshua always got a big kick out of telling this story.

Billy also related a story that William Joshua told him about traveling from Giles County Tennessee to Florence by driving a wagon. William Joshua said that it would take two or three days.

Billy still has vivid memories of William Joshua Rogers' general store. He relayed how cheese came in hoops and William Joshua had a cheese cutter and would slice off whatever his customers wanted. He would slice off a nickel or dime's worth or whatever they ordered and weigh it up.

Chewing tobacco came in large flat sheets back then. William Joshua also had a device to cut off whatever the customer wanted and would charge for it by weight.

Lard would also be weighed and sold by the pound. Customers would bring their own small buckets or other containers for it.

Saltine crackers also were sold by weight back then as they also came in bulk.

Billy also remembers that William Joshua traded in cotton and would store bales of cotton each year until the price increased enough that he could make a profit. One year he had two barns stuffed full of baled cotton. The price went down that year instead of going up as usual. Billy never knew just how much money that William Joshua lost that year but he does know that the loss was huge!

Immediately following are some receipts from 1898, 1899 and 1901 from William
Joshua Rogers' general store.

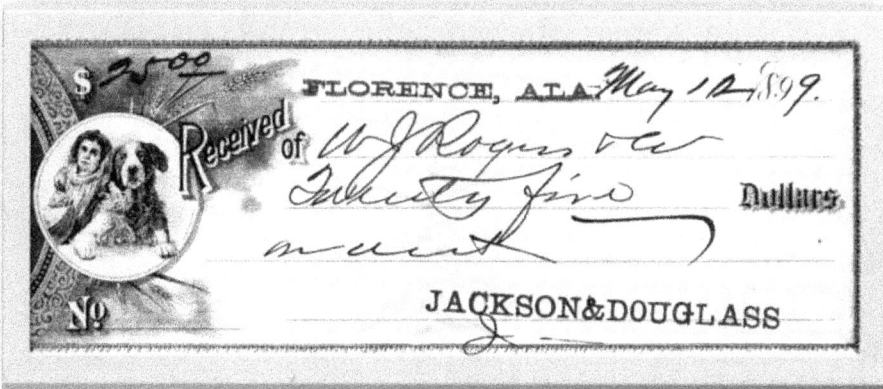

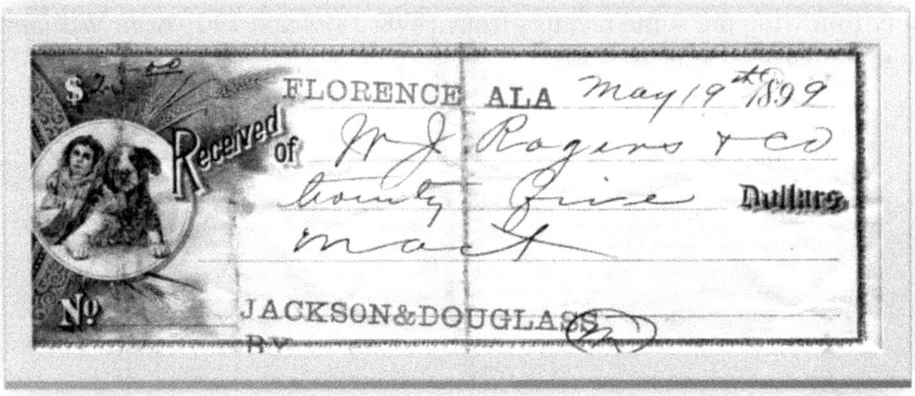

$2.00

FLORENCE, ALA May 19th 1899

Received of W J Rogers & Co

twenty five Dollars

mad

JACKSON & DOUGLASS

No

By

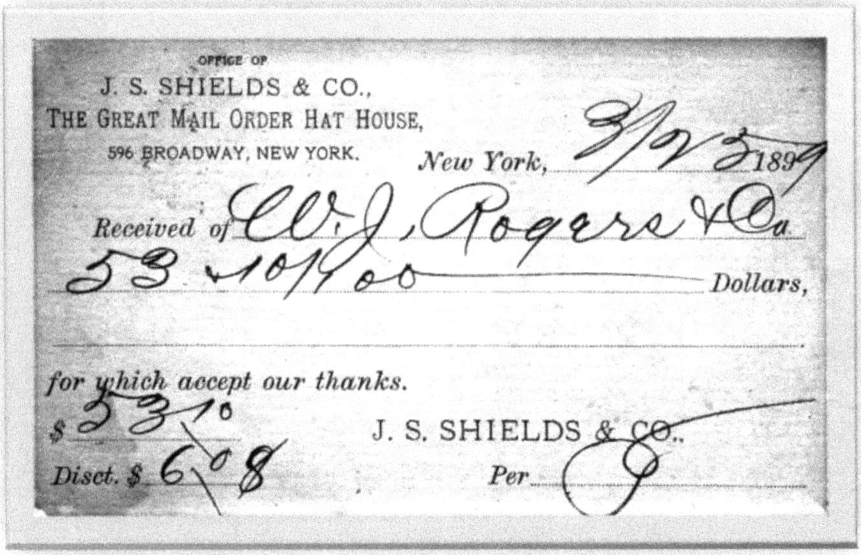

OFFICE OF

J. S. SHIELDS & CO.,

THE GREAT MAIL ORDER HAT HOUSE,

596 BROADWAY, NEW YORK.   New York, 3/V 3 1899

Received of W J Rogers & Co

53 10/00 Dollars,

for which accept our thanks.

$53 10   J. S. SHIELDS & CO.,

Disct. $ 6 08   Per

52

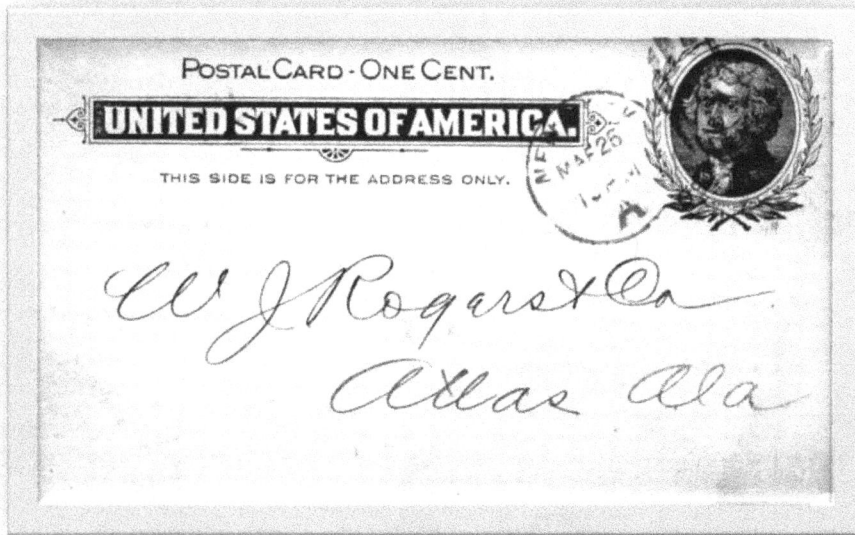

Penny postcard from 1899

I finally realized that William was a regularly used name during this time frame and keeps reappearing from generation to generation among these families and other families. The name Joshua was a fairly common name back in this time frame also. I can well understand the confusion on the internet for the various Joshua James' as well as William Joshua Rogers.

This pretty much ended my internet search and internet genealogical project. There was either too much and confusing or not enough information available on the internet for me to reach a reasonably accurate conclusion.

Part II

Tying Internet Research together With Family Stories

Chapter 9

Rogers' Family Stories

During my later visits with Billy and Doris Rogers, they let me take their documentation home to study and make copies. What they have is quite extensive and a lot of it was compiled and written by a family friend.

It was quickly apparent to me that the information that Finney Gray was referring to in conversations and what Billy Rogers had were two different documents. What Finney Gray told me about was supposedly only a few pages long and contained a copy of a newspaper article and what Billy Rogers has is quite extensive.

Billy and Doris Rogers' information does contain handwritten accounts of the family history written by two of Billy's aunts: Clara Rogers Clemons and Ona Rogers. The author thinks these documents are much more substantive than all of his internet research as these ladies were the granddaughters of Stephen H. Rogers. I know that they heard stories about the family from their father William Joshua Rogers (Stephen H. Rogers' son). Clara's information is quite complete and it was scanned in her own handwriting, while she could still write, and is included next with Billy's approval.

The mark ups on the document were apparently made by their family friend who had access to it for their work.

Rogers

One of the early merchants of the Atlas Beat was William Joshua Rogers, born 1859 in (1860 census) Rogersville, Al.

William's father, Stephen Rogus 1832 married 1837 Elvira James DC 1838 2 (daughter of Joshua + Esther James) They had one son, William Joshua Rogus.

His father, Stephen was a Confederate soldier and died in Rebel prison camp during the Civil war. Elvira, Williams mother died at age 24 and left William, an orphan at nine month's of age. His grandparents, the James, took William and later adopted him (and because of the trouble with Jesse + Frank James, (Joshua's nephews) William was permitted to wear the Rogers name.

William came to live in Atlas and married Matilda Hill 1868 (daughter of Bunn + Rebecca Barnett Hill)

Later, William's grandparents, the James house burned in Rogersville, and they came to live in Atlas, and settled about four miles south of Greenhill, which is now Hiway 43. They bought land, where they lived until 1881 and both died and are buried at Hill Cemetary

William Inherited land from his grandparents and built a small store 1890. He sold merchandise and traded with his Customers for Chickens, eggs, Butter, Corn, Molasses, scrap cotton and cotton which he hauled to be made into bales to the John Hill gin. He hauled the other products to Florence in a two horse wagon to be sold to other merchants, which was about a 12 hour trip, he usually carried one of his children with him, which was a great trip for them.

Later, he enlarged his store, and kept it until his death 1946 (1948 tombstone) and then the family Continued it until 1962

The land was later sold and now Donnie's market is just beside the old store and homeplace.

Some of the early Customers of the store were Joe McGee, Tom Thompson, Johnsy Harris, George Wallace, Terry Clemmons, Albert Tidwell George Haygood, Bose McGee, Guy Vaughn Morris Kingsly, Billy Beden, Walt Danly, Frank Thigpen, Jim Comer, Jim Frye, Billy Parker and many others. (355 words)

March 1998

Clara Rogers Clemons
Hwy 43- 4871
Killen

Tel. 757-2642

57

The document from Ona Rogers was written on the back of a blank check and was in her own handwriting. It contains information about the death of Stephen H. Rogers.

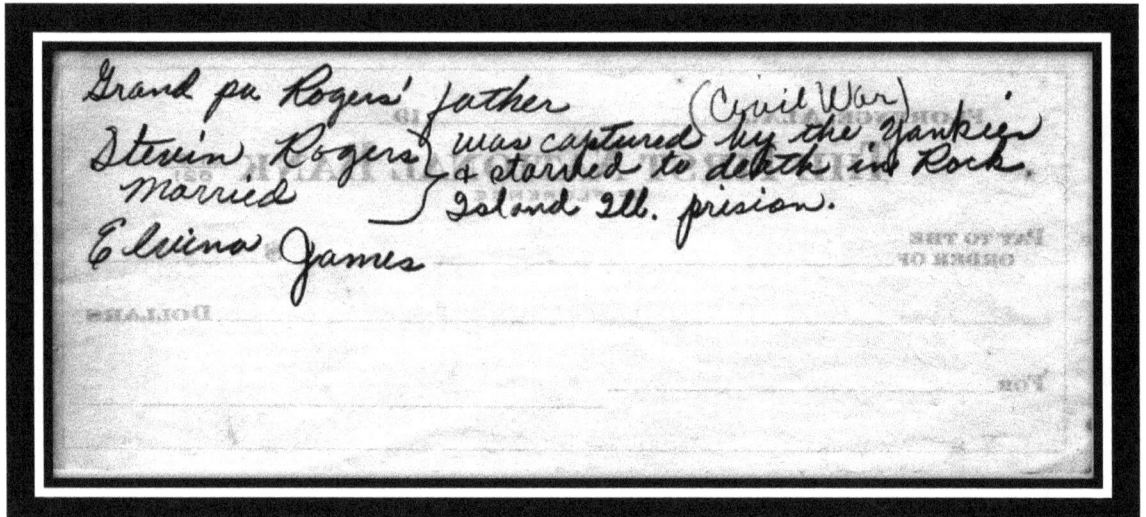

It should be noted that Clara Rogers Clemons referred to the fact that Jesse and Frank James were the nephews of Joshua James in her first page.

Billy's family friend traced Joshua James father to a Bennett James 1764 but did not mention their source. I could find no mention of a Bennett James in this time frame on the internet, certainly not one tied in with the family of Zerelda Cole and Robert Sallee James. I did find several Bennett James in later time periods. This does not mean that the connection is not true. The internet is silent about far too many things. These original documents are too close to the source to be ignored.

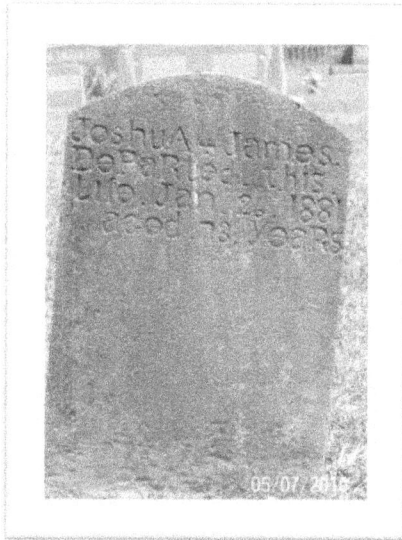

Grave marker of **Joshua James, Jr.** Hill Cemetery

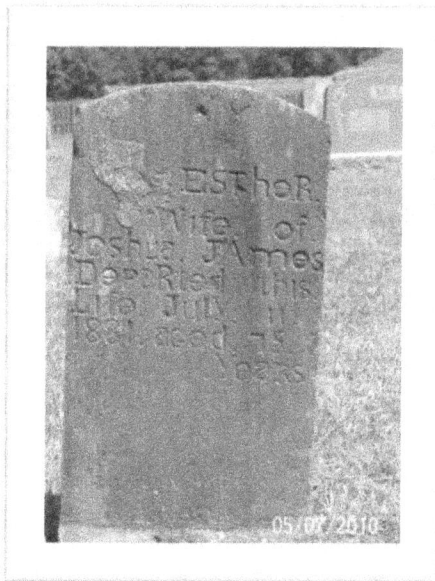

The grave marker of **Esther Hicks James**, Hill Cemetery.

The grave marker of **William Joshua Rogers and wife Matilda M. Hill Rogers**, Hill Cemetery, Bridge Road near Killen, Alabama.

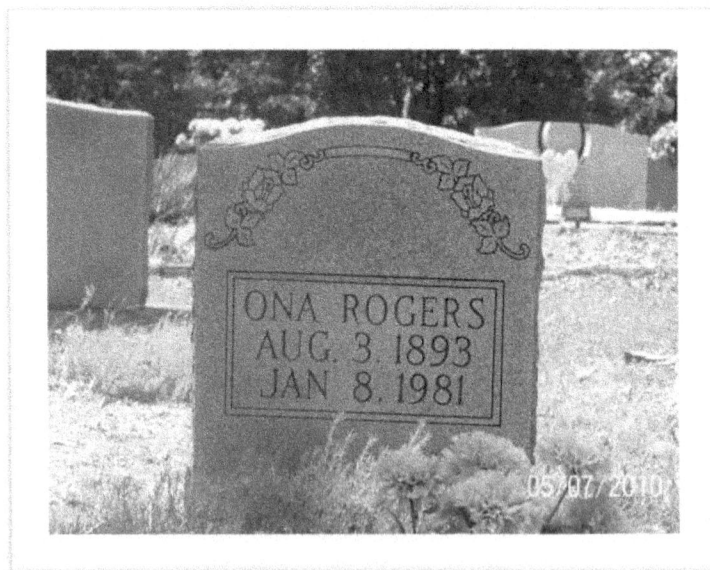

The grave marker of **Ona Rogers**, Hill Cemetery.

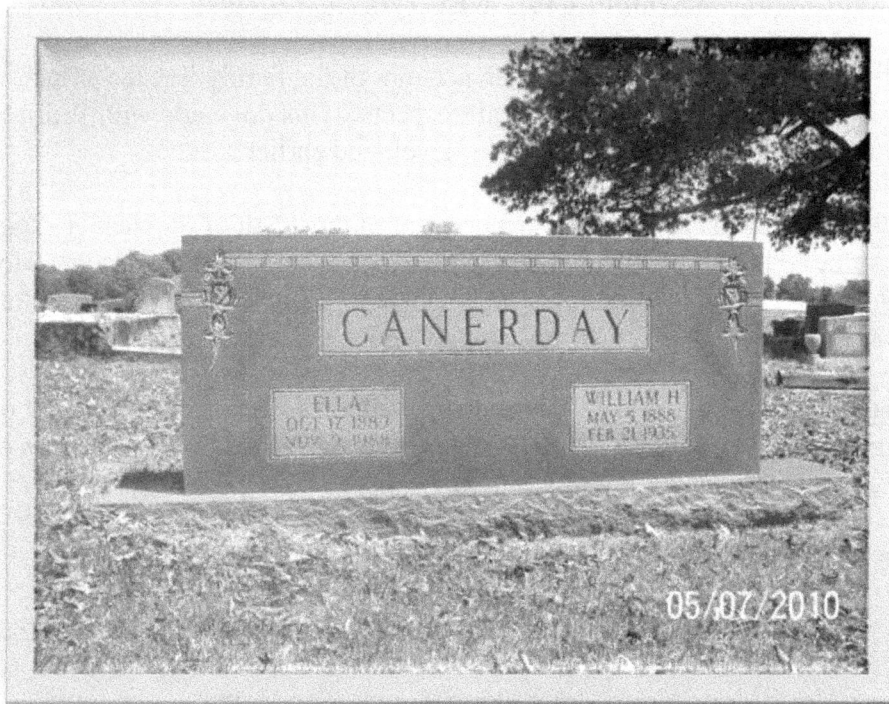

The grave marker of **Ella Rogers Canerday**, Hill Cemetery.

Chapter 10

Attempting to Tie Everything Together

1. I will take Clara Rogers' handwritten account of the family lineage at face value and will assume that it is correct in all respects. This dovetails with William Joshua Rogers' **Scenario I** which was developed earlier.

2. I will also take Ona Rogers' written account of the death of Stephen H. Rogers at face value. This means that he died in the Rock Island, Illinois Prisoner of war camp and not at the Prisoner of War stockade in Elmira, New York as indicated on the internet.

3. If **Scenario I** is taken as the true account, William Joshua Rogers account of having come out of Giles County, Tennessee is explained by Billy Rogers of him living in an orphanage for a time.

Next are the grave marker inscriptions of Joshua and Esther Hicks James.

The inscription on **Joshua James** grave marker reads:

Joshu A James
DePaRted this
Life. Jan. 26 1881
Aged. 73. YeaRs

Joshua James died January 26, 1881 and the Muscle Shoals payroll robbery did not happen until April 11, 1881. Joshua James was 73 years old when he died. This would mean that he was born about 1808 and would have been about twelve years old when he arrived in the Rogersville, Alabama area by flatboat with Joshua James, Sr. in 1820.

The inscription on **Esther Hicks James** grave marker reads:

ESTheR
Wife of
Joshua. James

DepaRted this
Life. July. 11.
1881. Aged. 75.
Years

Esther Hicks James did not die until July 11, 1881 which was three months after the robbery took place. Esther was about 75 years old when she died. This would mean that she was born about 1806 and would have been about fourteen years old when she arrived in the Rogersville, Alabama area by flatboat with Joshua James, Sr.

Could Frank and Jesse James have been checking on their aged and failing relatives in Alabama while they were also making plans for the Muscle Shoals payroll robbery?

4.   If Joshua James was the uncle of Frank and Jesse James, William Joshua Rogers would have interacted with them only as a young lad. Frank James was born on January 10, 1843 and Jesse James was born in 1847 and they were of the same generation as Joshua James' children listed as follows:

Sarah C. James born about 1832.
Harriet S. James born about 1833 in Alabama.
Mary James born about 1834 in Alabama.
Elvira I. James born about 1835 in Alabama.
Isabella James born about 1838 in Alabama.
Richard James born about 1842 in Alabama.
Joshua L. James born about 1845 in Alabama.
California James born about 1848 in Alabama.

The inscription on **Sarah C. James'** grave marker reads:

Sarah C. James
Wife of
A. G. Hill
July 23, 1830
March 10, 1906

The inscription on **Harriett S. James'** grave marker reads:

HARRIETT S.
Daughter of Joshua and Esther
James
Born Feb. (25?) 1852
Died
Oct. 11. 1853

The grave marker for Harriett S. James was made of marble. The others for the Joshua James- Esther Hicks James family were made of what appears to have been limestone or it was poor quality marble that has eroded away somewhat.

The inscription on **Elvira I. James'** grave marker reads:

Elvira I. Consort of
S. H. Rogers & Daughter
Of J. & Esther James.
Died Aug. 4th 1861
Aged about 24 years.

If Elvira was about 24 when she died in 1861, she would have been born about 1837.

5. William Joshua Rogers was listed in the 1880 U. S. Census at age 19 as living with Joshua James and Esther Hicks James. Both Joshua James and Esther Hicks James died in 1881. Could this be when William Joshua Rogers went to the orphanage in Giles County, Tennessee? Or could it have had something to do with the Muscle Shoals payroll robbery that happened about the same time?

The author next tried to pick up any information that he could find on the internet about either L. D. Holloway or Morgan Matthews hoping to find the identity of the person or persons who had taken them in as young men in Giles County, Tennessee but to no avail. The fathomless black bog of time would not divulge any more of its secrets about this matter! William Joshua Rogers was the only one of the group that he could find any information about on the internet. This also ended his internet research for this project...*for now.*

Author's note - Morgan Matthews was finally located in a U. S. Census report of 1870 listing him living in the Joshua James household in Atlas, Lauderdale County, Alabama, at age 9. This is probably where he and William Joshua Rogers became friends and went to the orphanage in Giles County, Tennessee together.

Chapter 11

I was still not completely satisfied with the confusing information about all of the different Joshua James' that had been unearthed. I had to let all of this percolate and settle in my mind for several weeks. It seems that I often do my best thinking about any perplexing problem that faces me while asleep! I awakened one morning with a single thought in my mind – What did William Lindsey McDonald have to say about Joshua James in his book, *A Walk Through the Past,* – if anything?

William Lindsey McDonald wrote this book and it was published in 1997. It was reprinted in 2003 by Bluewater Publications. This is a very well written and documented book in which William McDonald interviewed countless people and it includes numerous places and people of Florence and Lauderdale County, Alabama. It is an excellent reference book for anyone interested in the early happenings and people of the Shoals area.

William McDonald did mention Joshua James, as well as his father, Joshua James Sr., and gives the following account on page 238:

"Baptist minister Joshua James, Senior., was among the early settlers (of Rogersville). According to legend, James was sent by a Baptist church in Boston, Massachusetts, to work with the Indians. His family arrived on a flatboat at Lamb's Ferry around 1820. His daughter-in-law, Esther, organized the town's first school in a log house on Lamb's Ferry Road. Joshua James, Senior, is buried in the Liberty Cemetery in Rogersville. The graves of Joshua, Junior and Esther are in the Jones-Hill Cemetery near Florence."

I found an updated survey of the Liberty Cemetery in Rogersville, Alabama and have located the cemetery. The first survey was done in 1995 by Mary Lois Graham and Eleatha Howard and was updated in 2006 by Bob Torbert. The cemetery is so old that the older grave markers are almost unreadable.

Joshua James, Sr. was reportedly buried in this cemetery but is not listed in either survey. It is noted in *Cemeteries Of East Lauderdale County Alabama*, published in

1996 by The Friends Of The Rogersville Public Library of which Billy Rogers has a copy and I quote Mary Lois Graham and Eleatha Howard literally.

"This cemetery is about two blocks from downtown Rogersville on West Lee Street. This cemetery contains many large areas of vacant spaces that appear to be graves. They are not marked in any way. The first settlers of the area built a brush arbor as a place of worship where this cemetery is now located. The arbor was built by Baptists but all faiths worshiped there. Local families began to bury around the church. The cemetery was named for the old church. This is believed to be one of the oldest cemeteries in the area.

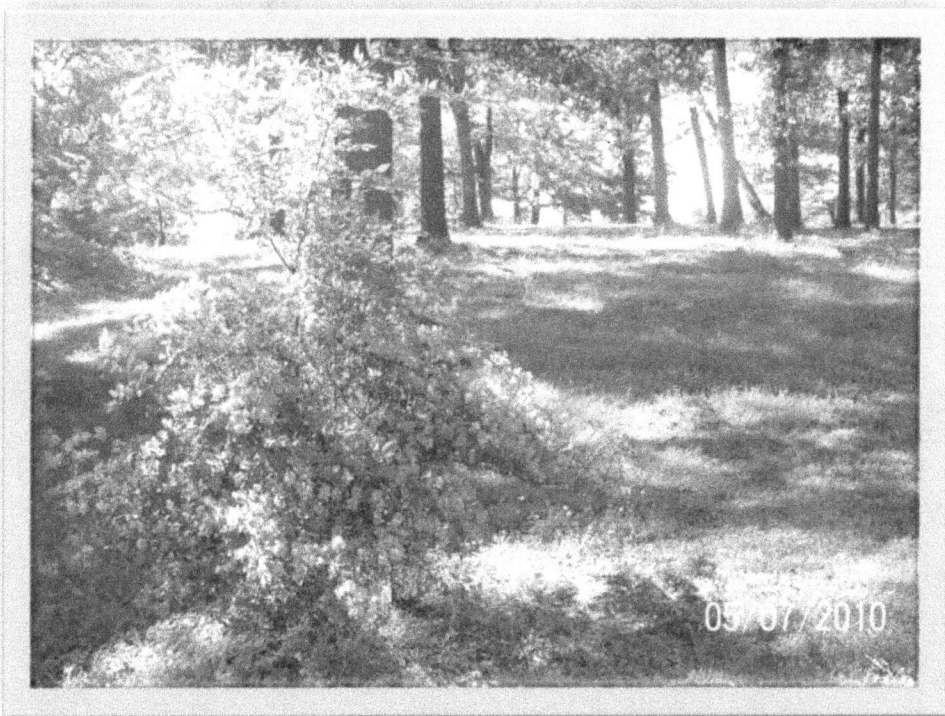

View of the **Liberty Cemetery** in Rogersville, Alabama looking south.

View of the **Liberty Cemetery** in Rogersville, Alabama looking north. Two of Joshua James, Junior and Esther Hicks James daughters are buried here. Harriett S. James and Elvira I. James Rogers are listed on both of the referenced surveys.

Grave markers for **Elvira I. James Rogers**, left, and **Harriett S. James**, right. The grave marker for Harriett S. James is broken. Liberty Cemetery.

Close-up of **Elvira I. James'** grave marker showing the inscription, Liberty Cemetery.

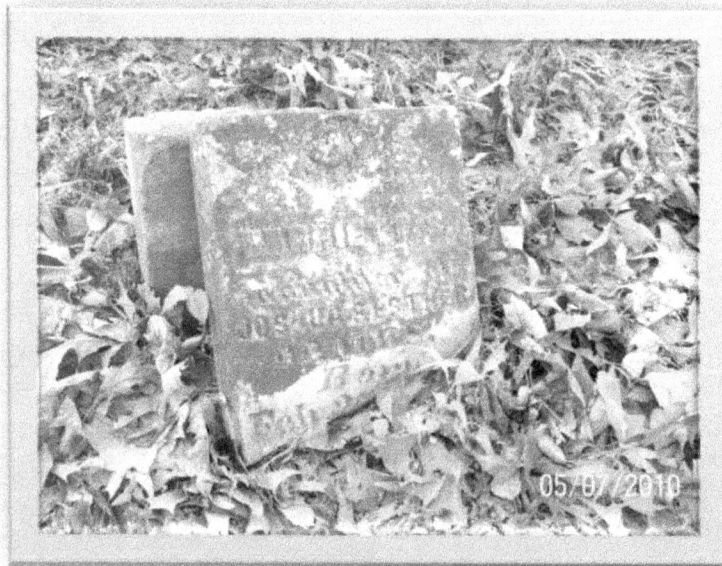

Top part of Harriett S. James' grave marker, Liberty Cemetery.

Bottom portion of Harriett S. James' grave marker. Liberty Cemetery.

In paragraph 2 on page 98, William McDonald gives the following account of the activities of Frank and Jesse James in this area. He is discussing a canal around the shoals that blocked river traffic both above and below the muscle shoals on the Tennessee River. "A railroad track was built alongside the canal. A locomotive known as "the Little Train" towed boats through the canal. The observation coach pulled by the engine was known as the "Black Maria."

Jesse and Frank James, with Wild Bill Ryan, robbed the paymaster from the Blue Water Creek Construction Camp on March 11, 1881. This official had gone to Florence to pick up the weekly payroll. On his return to the camp the James gang took the entire $5,000 he was carrying.

Lock Six near Killen was the headquarters of the Muscle Shoals Canal. This beautifully landscaped reservation became a popular visitor's paradise. Author and English Professor Joshua Nicholas Winn, III (I went to Coffee High School in Florence with his son, Nicholas Winn.) who was reared at Muscle Shoals often referred to it as the garden spot of the world." I also took an English class from Professor Joshua Nicholas Winn at Florence State College at the time, now UNA. Mr. Winn was a marvelous teacher.

William McDonald also states on pages 241 and 242 while discussing Old Anderson:

"There are a number of old legends about this area of the county. One involves Jesse and Frank James who, according to a popular story, came to live with a relative during the winter of 1882. A burial site in an old cemetery near Anderson is known as "the grave of the daughter of Frank James." Ingrum Hollow is a few miles south of Anderson. The Ingrums moved their log house here from Calicoa in **Giles County**, Tennessee, a few years before Alabama became a state. They established a trading post alongside the Lamb's Ferry Road. This family found friendly Indians who taught the men how to save ammunition by hunting with bows and arrows. These native Americans spoke of a great earthquake – perhaps the New Madrid Earthquake of 1811 – which caused a part of the nearby bluff to fall into Anderson Creek. William Franklin Ingrum, Sr., later built a grist mill, wool carding mill, rolling mill, blacksmith shop, and general store in Ingrum Hollow. During the Civil War they moved their log house to this hollow to escape the Yankees who were frequently on the road between Pulaski and Rogersville. A line of old trenches can be seen above this hollow. It is believed they were placed at this strategic place to defend the approach from Lamb's Ferry Road."

Author's note - According to Clara Rogers Clemons earlier referenced information, Joshua James and Esther Hicks James had moved to the Atlas area earlier to live after their house burned and both died in 1881 and were buried in the Hill cemetery near Greenhill, Alabama. Due to complications after the 1881 Muscle Shoals payroll robbery, Frank and Jesse James could not possibly have been in Alabama in the winter of 1882.

1. Jesse was killed in Missouri in April of 1882.

2. Frank surrendered in Missouri in October 1882.

Using the information from William Lindsey McDonald's book, I reasoned that Joshua James, Senior, must have had connections in Massachusetts and there could be information about **this Joshua James** on Ancestry.com and Familysearch.org. The following pedigree was established for him. It is not the only one that could have been developed from the information available on the internet but was the most plausible one that I thought could be developed for him. The earliest person named in this pedigree was **John James** and is reconstructed as follows:

John James born about 1720, no other information was given on OneWorldTree. There were several John James' listed in the early linage of Frank and Jesse James and the James family was very prolific.

Married

Prudence Stanton born on Dear Island, Maine, USA. Died 6 August 1740 in Scituate, Plymouth, Massachusetts.

Children

James Stanton	M	13 October 1738 in Scituate, Plymouth, Massachusetts.
Prudence James	F	28 December 1740 in Scituate, Plymouth, Massachusetts.
Rhoda James	F	29 December 1742 in Scituate, Plymouth, Massachusetts.
Elisha James Massachusetts.	**M**	**13 August 1774 in Scituate, Plymouth,**
Eunice James	F	3 March 1747 in Scituate, Plymouth, Massachusetts.
Lydia James	F	27 November 1749 in Scituate, Plymouth, Massachusetts.
Lucy James	F	8 October 1751 in Scituate, Plymouth, Massachusetts.
Thomas James	M	9 June 1753 in Scituate, Plymouth, Massachusetts.

The following is from Familysearch.org:

Elisha James Born 13 August 1744 in Scituate, Plymouth, Massachusetts.

Married 1774 in Scituate, Plymouth, Massachusetts.

Sarah Foster Born about 1752 in Scituate, Plymouth, Massachusetts.

Sarah (Ruth in another entry) Foster
Born 1749 in Scituate, Plymouth, Massachusetts.

In another entry Ruth Foster had three husbands:
1. Nathan Crittenden.
2. Nathaniel Crittenden
3. Elisha James.

Children

>Elisha James
>Born about 1776 in Scituate, Plymouth, Massachusetts.
>
>Temperance James (Female)
>Born about 1782 in Scituate, Plymouth, Massachusetts.
>
>**Joshua James** (Male)
>Born about 1785 (1780 in another entry, 20 June 1787 in yet another) in Scituate, Plymouth, Massachusetts.

No information about Joshua James other than this was listed. No information on his wife's name or the number and names of children are available from this search on Familysearch.org or could be found on Ancestry.com. This probably started all of the confusion listed earlier in this project. This would mean that Joshua James was about 40 when he arrived at Lamb's Ferry in Lauderdale County, Alabama.

Joshua James, Sr. and Junior both apparently arrived in the Shoals Area in about 1820 along with Elvira Hicks James, according to William Lindsey McDonald.

Sidenote

A sidenote about William Lindsey McDonald and his tie in with our family. He was the pastor for a time at the Harrison Chapel Methodist Church and later became my sister, Ann Crittenden's supervisor at TVA.

He was visiting with the family once while my brother Nathan Keith Tidwell was having serious surgery at the Coffee Eliza Memorial Hospital in Florence, Alabama. He had this story to relate to me when he found out that I was currently living in Scottsboro.

As a young man fresh out of college he took a job with the Hinshaw Funeral Home in Scottsboro for a time. He told of an old gentleman who lived way back in one of the remote mountain coves that had died. For those who don't relate to our local definition of mountain cove, it is the flat land at the foot of the numerous mountains in our area.

Anyway, he and someone else hitched up the mules to the wagon they had to use to go and pick the old gentleman up with. He said they had to ford several creeks and streams to get back to where he lived.

They picked him up and brought him back to town where they cleaned him up and dressed him in a nice suit of clothes and did what they could to really fix him up properly and took him back home.

They went back to pick him up at the appointed time for the funeral and were utterly shocked at what they found. His clothes were all wrinkled, his hair was all messed up and the lining of the casket was torn. He looked like he had been in an awful fight!

They wondered what on earth had happened to him. One of the sons explained, "We had never seen Papa looking that pretty so we took him out and propped him up against the barn. We all gathered around him and had our picture taken!"

Bill McDonald was still chuckling about this after all of the years that had passed. I think that he was, and still is, a truly remarkable man. I could well relate to this story and appreciated all of the details he still remembered about it. I can understand why the congregation at Harrison's Chapel Church truly loved this man and he loved all of them as well.

Chapter 12

Preliminary Conclusion

Hold on folks! The story is not nearly complete. It's just starting to get interesting.

1. While the internet is a valuable tool for genealogical research, it cannot be relied on exclusively in a complex quest such as this one.

2. Family stories are also a valuable tool but distantly past family members can embellish these stories. I experienced this while doing research for my own family.

3. Other published sources are valuable tools as well, as illustrated by William Lindsey McDonald's work and how it tied in with this project. Unfortunately he acknowledged that he was repeating old and sometimes local legends regarding Joshua James, Sr. and Frank and Jesse James visiting a family member in the area.

4. All of these sources must be tied together for any meaningful conclusion to be formed.

5. What is really the truth about all of this? The reader must decide. I may well have missed something, and probably did, while sorting through all of the voluminous information that I dug up while working on this project. The reader may well have access to old family stories, legends and myths that were not available to me.

This project is but another illustration of why I encourage all readers to document their family stories now while a good portion of this information is still available. It will never be any fresher than it is right now! All that it will take for this information to switch from being facts to becoming legends and myths is for the loss of one family member or two who have this information in their minds right now.

At that point, the dark, endless and fathomless black bog of time will snatch it up forever. The infamous bog has never been known to give up much meaningful information.

After reviewing all of this data for yet another time I believe the following to be factual for the genealogy of the current Rogers and Gray families that were the subject of this project. Everything is well documented by internet research and most of it dovetails closely with family stories.

Chapter 13

Stephen H. Rogers Patriarchal Pedigree

Joseph Rogers, Sr.
> B. 1748

Joseph Rogers Jr.
> B. About 1776
> M. 13 October 1797 in Granville County, N.C.
> D. In Greenville County, N.C.

Married

Dora Dicey Kittrell born 1776 died 1851 on 14 October 1797 in Granville County, N.C.

Children
> Sarah Leah Rogers born 1798.
> **Samuel Rogers born 1799 in Granville County, N.C.**
> John Rogers born about 1800 in Granville County, N.C.
> Jonathan T. Rogers born about 1801 in Granville County, N.C.
> Martha Rogers born 1803.
> Rachael Rogers born about 1805 in Granville County, N.C.
> Mary Nancy Rogers born about 1813 in Granville County, N.C. died 1838.
> Willis Rogers born about 1819 in Granville County, N.C.

Samuel Rogers
> B. 1799 in Granville County, N.C.
> M. 4 January 1829 in Morgan County, Alabama.
> D. Lauderdale County, Alabama.

Married

Mary White
  B. 1800

Children

  Stephen H. Rogers
  B. 1832 in Rogersville, Lauderdale County, Alabama.
  D. 1864 in a POW prison.

Stephen H. Rogers
  B. 1832 in Rogersville, Lauderdale County, Alabama.
  D. 1864 at Elmira, New York. (Rock Island Illinois?) POW prison.

Married

Elvira I. James 1837-1861

Children

  William Joshua Rogers.
  B. December 1860 in Rogersville, Lauderdale County, Alabama.
  D. 1948 in Lauderdale County, Alabama.

William Joshua Rogers.
  B. December 1860 in Rogersville, Lauderdale County, Alabama.
  D. 1948 in Lauderdale County, Alabama.

Owned a general country mercantile store. His daughter Ona ran the store in later years.

Married

Matilda W. M. Hill 1862-1954 in 1888 in Lauderdale County Alabama.

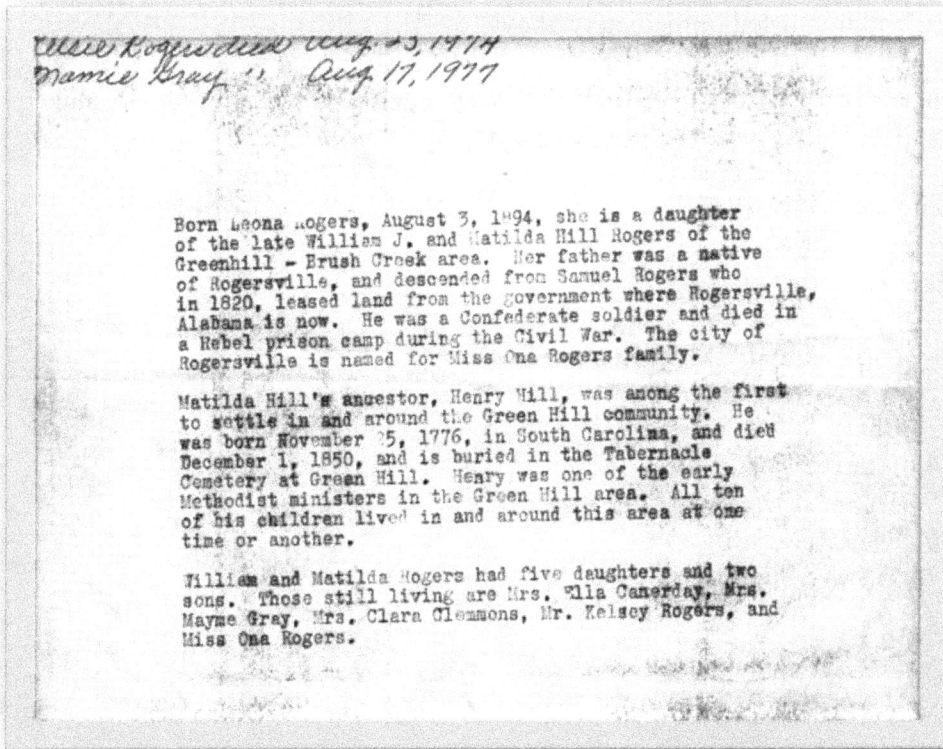

Born Leona Rogers, August 3, 1894, she is a daughter of the late William J. and Matilda Hill Rogers of the Greenhill - Brush Creek area. Her father was a native of Rogersville, and descended from Samuel Rogers who in 1820, leased land from the government where Rogersville, Alabama is now. He was a Confederate soldier and died in a Rebel prison camp during the Civil War. The city of Rogersville is named for Miss Ona Rogers family.

Matilda Hill's ancestor, Henry Hill, was among the first to settle in and around the Green Hill community. He was born November 25, 1776, in South Carolina, and died December 1, 1850, and is buried in the Tabernacle Cemetery at Green Hill. Henry was one of the early Methodist ministers in the Green Hill area. All ten of his children lived in and around this area at one time or another.

William and Matilda Rogers had five daughters and two sons. Those still living are Mrs. Ella Canerday, Mrs. Mayme Gray, Mrs. Clara Clemmons, Mr. Kelsey Rogers, and Miss Ona Rogers.

An old Rogers' family document discussing Matilda Hill and some of her children.

Children

1. Ella Rogers Canerday 1889-1988
2. Ona Rogers 1889-1981
3. Sallie Rebecca Rogers 1891-1914
4. Leona Rogers 1893-1981
5. **Ira Norman Rogers 1898-1969**
6. **Mayme Esther Rogers 1900-1977. Married Gus Gray and is Finney Gray's mother along with several other children.**
7. William Kilsey Rogers 1904-1974
8. Clara Rogers Clemmons 1907-2009

There is not much information on the internet for William Joshua and Matilda Rogers' children listed immediately above.

Ira Norman Rogers born April 19,1898 in Lauderdale County Alabama, died October 1969 in Killen, Lauderdale County Alabama.

Married **Clara Mae Hill**.

Children from this marriage:

1. Paris Arnold "Billy" Rogers
2. Francis Josephine "Jo" Rogers
3. Charles Oran Rogers
4. John Ira Rogers
5. Thomas Eugene "Tom" Rogers
6. Robert Don Rogers
7. Marilyn Sue Rogers

Chapter 14

The following information came to light while I was researching material that Ronald Pettus had let me borrow as material to draw from in our writer's group while attempting to write a play about the March 11, 1881 Muscle Shoals Payroll robbery near present day Killen, Alabama.

While reviewing this information, I noticed that one of the witnesses at the Frank James trial was one Alfred G. Hill of the Atlas community. I ran a quick and dirty internet search for information on him and found that his full name was Alfred Green Hill. This implication did not fully register at first but as I usually do while facing a perplexing problem, I kept mulling over it in my sleep. I awoke one morning with the thought in my mind – Alfred Green Hill – Green Hill – is there any connection with him and the town of Greenhill Alabama? It turned out that there was but the town was supposedly named after his uncle, Green Berry Hill!

This peaked my interest and knowing that both the Rogers and Gray families had connections with the Hill family led me to a more extensive internet search.

This, and some of the information that Ronald Pettus shared with me, also revealed that some of the happenings before, during and after the Muscle Shoals payroll robbery might tie in with what I had done so far in trying to tie in the Rogers and Gray families with the family of Frank and Jesse James.

I will start with Alfred Green Hill's family listed in various family trees in **Ancestry.com:**

Alfred Green Hill born October 17, 1825 in Carthage, Moore County, North Carolina, died September 27, 1898 in Lauderdale County, Alabama.

Married 1st **Lucinda Woods** 1822-1856 on August 11, 1847 in Lauderdale County, Alabama. The couple was living at Division 2 East of the Military Road in Lauderdale County, Alabama in 1850.

Children:

> James H. Hill 1848-1849.
> John Hill 1850-1923.
> Orlando Hill 1853-
> Son Hill 1856-1856.

Married 2nd **Lydia Harnell Harrison** 1828-1873 on December 28, 1856 in Lauderdale County, Alabama.

Children:

> Infant Hill 1856-1856.
> Banjamin Franklin Hill 1856-1914.
> Olive Hill 1857-1928.
> Alfretta Hill 1859-1927.
> Sarah Arlla Hill 1861-
> Alfred Hugh Hill 1864-1916.
> Henry Augustus Hill 1866-1936
> Lee Hill 1872-

Married 3rd after 1873 **Sara C. James** 1830-1906 age 48. Sarah C. James was the daughter of Joshua James, Junior and Esther Hicks James.

Grave marker of **Alfred Green Hill**, Hill Cemetery, Bridge Road near Killen, Alabama.

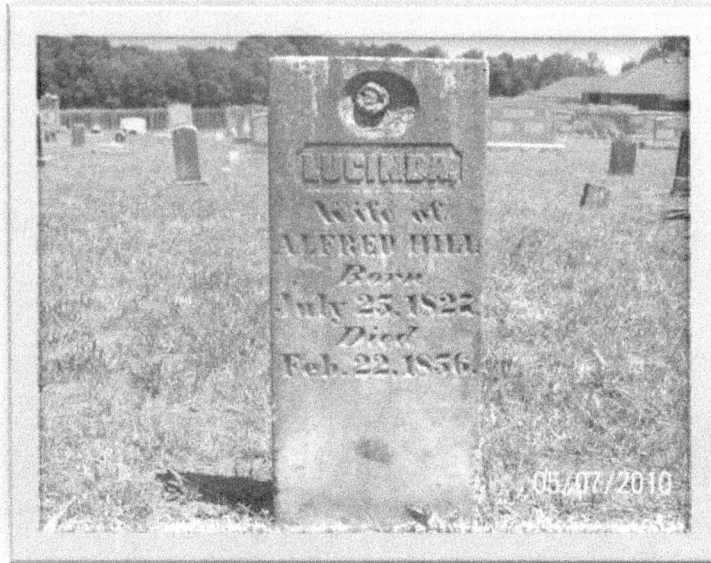

Grave marker of **Lucinda Hill**, Hill Cemetery.

Grave marker of **Lydia Hill**, Hill Cemetery.

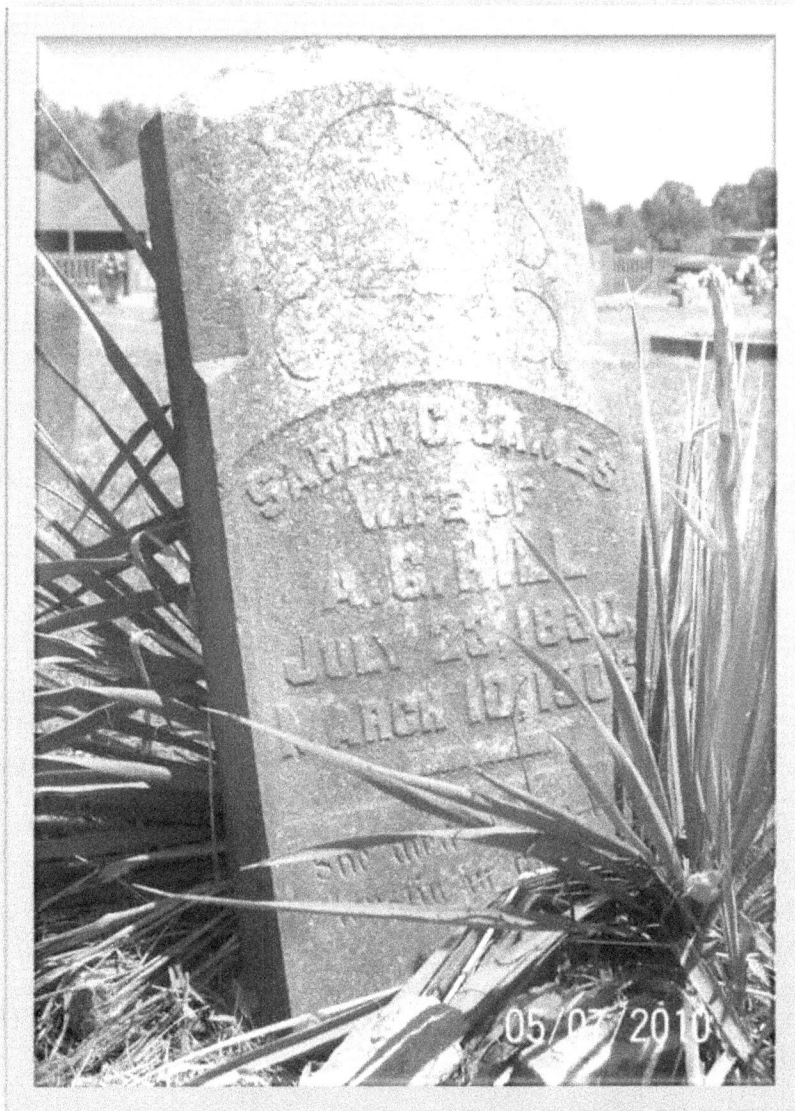

Grave marker of **Sarah C. James Hill**, Hill Cemetery.

The following details the pedigrees of all of the associated families with the Rogers and Gray families, then we will get back to the story. This should add some richness to the family history. It will also demonstrate how so few people back in the 1700s can result into such large families now and how they intermix and intertwine.

The following is a compilation of information from Familysearch.org, Ancestry.com including the P-Murray tree and interviews with Paris A. (Billy) Rogers.

Hill - Stutts - McMurtrey Pedigree

I. Hiram Hill born 1774 in Carthage, Moore County, North Carolina, died 1855 in Killen, Lauderdale County, Alabama.

Married **Hyrum Hill** 1776-1850. Hyrum was born about 1776 in Carthage, Moore County, North Carolina and died about 1850 in Lauderdale County, Alabama.

Children:

> Martin Hill 1795-1849. Born in Carthage, Moore County, North Carolina.
> Amy Hill 1795-. Born in Carthage, Moore County, North Carolina.
> Mary Polly Hill was born about 1798 in Carthage, Moore County, North Carolina.
> **James Hill** 1798-1878.
> Green Berry Hill* 1803-1852.
> Nancy Hill 1804-. Born in Carthage, Moore County, North Carolina.
> Matilda (Mary) Sousannah Hill** 1808-1914. She was born on February 17, 1808 in Carthage, Moore County, North Carolina.

* The town of Greenhill in Lauderdale County, Alabama was supposedly named for **Green Berry Hill**.

** **Matilda Sousannah Hill** is listed twice as being the daughter of both Hiram Hill and James Hill.

The following is according to the P. Murray tree on Ancestry.com.

II. James Hill born 1798 in Carthage, Moore County, North Carolina, died February 28, 1878 in Killen, Lauderdale County, Alabama. Buried in the Hill cemetery near Greenhill, Alabama.

Married **Catherine Stutts** 1825 in Carthage, Moore County, North Carolina. Catherine was born on November 16, 1802 at Carthage, Moore County, North Carolina, died on September 21, 1872.

Children:

Alfred Green Hill 1825-1898***.
William Hiram Hill 1827-1888.
Archibald Hill 1829-1904.
Sara Elizabeth Hill 1832-1923.
Martha Adeline Hill 1834-1915.
Jacob Hill 1837-1862.
Matilda Sousannah Hill**1838-1914.
Nancy Bell Hill 1841-1878.

*** Alfred Green Hill testified at the Frank James April 1884 trial in Huntsville, Alabama. According to The Huntsville Historical Review, Vol 2, April 1972, Number 2, page 12 by Leland R. Johnson and part of Ronald Pettus' Archives, that three men stayed at his house north of the canal before the robbery and made inquiry about the date the canal employees were paid. Neither he nor another witness Hugh Riley, bartender at Peden's saloon, could do more than say that Frank James resembled one of the men.

***III. **William Hiram Hill** born September 17, 1827 in Moore County North Carolina, died February 6, 1888 in Lauderdale County, Alabama. Buried in the Hill Cemetery, Lauderdale County, Alabama.

Military Company E, 27th Alabama Infantry, C.S.A.

Married Rebecca Barrett 1833-1921

Children:

James A. Hill 1856-1940.
Lucinda Hill 1858-1930. Married Batch McMurtrey- Cecil McMurtrey's grandfather.
Cynthia Hill 1860-1945.

Matilda Hill 1864-1954.
Sarah (Sally) Hill 1866-1923
John J. Hill 1868-1950.
Viola Hill Wilson.
Rebecca Hill 1/122/1873-7/2 1873.

IV. Matilda Hill 1864-1954 married **William Joshua Rogers** in 1888 in Lauderdale County, Alabama.

Children:

Ella Rogers 1889-
Ona Rogers 1889-
Sallie Rebecca Rogers 1891-1914.
Leona Rogers 1892-1981.
Ira Norman Rogers 1898-1969.
Mayme Esther Rogers 1900-1977.
William Kilsey Rogers 1904-1974.
Clara Rogers 1907-2009.

Catherine Stutts Pedigree

A. Jacobus Heinrich Stutts born May 29, 1732 in Moore County, North Carolina. Died 1796 in Moore County, North Carolina.

Married 1st **Elizabeth Barrett**.

One child.

George Washington Stutts 1833-1897.

Married 2nd **Elizabeth J. Stutts** 1732-1796. One child:

Leonard Stutts 1765-1856.

B. Leonard Stutts born 1765 in Moore County, North Carolina, died November 20, 1856 in Lauderdale County, Alabama.

Married

Mary Williamson 1775-1845 in Moore County, North Carolina.

Their residence in 1850 was Division 2 East of the Military Road, Lauderdale County, Alabama.

Children:

1. Jacob Stutts 1797-1885.
2. William M. Stutts 1798-1883.
3. **Catherine Stutts 1802-1872.**
4. Leonard Martin Stutts 1805-1856.
5. Susan Stutts 1806-1898.
6. Elizabeth Stutts 1807-1899.
7. Mary Stutts 1810-1855.
8. Henry Stutts 1814-1885.
9. Christian Christopher Stutts 1815-1866.
10. Anderson Stutts 1816-1911.
11. Kendrick Stutts 1817-1905.

C. Catherine Stutts born November 16, 1802 in Carthage, Moore County, North Carolina, died September 21, 1872 in Killen, Lauderdale County, Alabama.

Married 1825 **James Hill** born 1798 in Carthage, Moore County, North Carolina, died February 28, 1878 in Killen, Lauderdale County, Alabama, in Carthage, Moore County, North Carolina.

Chapter 15

Ira Norman Rogers and Mayme Esther Rogers Gray Family

Ira Norman Rogers born April 19, 1898 in Lauderdale County, Alabama, died October 14, 1969 in Killen, Lauderdale County, Alabama.

Married **Clara Mae Hill.**

Children:

1. Paris Arnold "Billy" Rogers born December 15, 1922 in Atlas Community, Lauderdale County, Alabama. Married Doris Laverne Spears on January 4, 1947. Four children: two surviving sons and a daughter all live in the Shoals area.
2. Francis Josephine "Jo" Rogers born May 6, 1925 in Atlas Community, Lauderdale County, Alabama. Died May of 2010 in Nashville, Tennessee. Married William Lee Gray. Two daughters who are retired school teachers. One lives near Bradenton Florida and the other lives in the Brentwood area of Nashville, Tennessee.
3. Charles Oran Rogers born May 30, 1928 in Atlas Community, Lauderdale County, Alabama. Married Dorothy Fay Davis. Charles died in Houston Texas on April 18, 2008. Three children who all live in Texas.
4. John Ira Rogers born October 7, 1931 in Atlas Community, Lauderdale County, Alabama. Married Imogine Barnett. Two children who live in the Huntsville, Alabama area.
5. Thomas Eugene "Tom" Rogers born July 10, 1933 in Atlas Community, Lauderdale County, Alabama. Married Dorothy Louise Crosswhite. Thomas died in Killen, Alabama on December 4, 2005. Two children: a boy and a girl.
6. Robert Don Rogers born May 27, 1935 in Atlas Community, Lauderdale County, Alabama. Married Willie Idell Lovelace. Two daughters: one lives in Hartselle Alabama and the other lives in Florence.

7. Marilyn Sue Rogers born December 20, 1937 in Atlas Community, Lauderdale County, Alabama. Married Donald England Raney. Two children: a son and daughter who live in the Decatur, Alabama area.

Mayme Esther Rogers Family

Mayme Esther Rogers, daughter of William Joshua Rogers and Matilda Hill Rogers, was born October 21, 1900 in Lauderdale County, Alabama, died August 23 1977 in Lauderdale County, Alabama. Mayme is buried in the North Carolina church cemetery near Greenhill, Alabama.

Married James Gus Gray after 1914 in Lauderdale County, Alabama at age 14. James Gus Gray was born on July 31 1887 in Lauderdale County, Alabama, died December 23, 1963 in Lauderdale County, Alabama and is buried in the North Carolina church cemetery near Greenhill, Alabama.

James Gus Gray married 1st

Liddie House in 1910 born February 24, 1890 in Lauderdale County, Alabama, died December 24, 1914 in Lauderdale County, Alabama. Liddie is buried in the North Carolina church cemetery near Greenhill, Alabama.

Children:

> Thomas Lee Gray born about 1911.
> Earl Hugh Gray born about 1914.

Married 2nd

Mayme Esther Rogers born October 21, 1900 in Lauderdale County, Alabama, died August 23, 1977 in Lauderdale County, Alabama. Buried in the North Carolina church cemetery near Greenhill Alabama.

Children:

> Helen Gray
> Kate Nell Gray.
> **Oscar Finney Gray**
> Logan Gray.
> Kenneth Gray.
> James C. Gray.
> Glen Gray.

Oscar Finney Gray born January 30, 1923, died October 8, 2005 from an extended battle with pneumonia.

Married **Reba Jane Tidwell** born November 13, 1927 died July 16, 2000 from complications of ALS.

Children:

> **Michael Finney Gray** born January 22, 1962 in Lauderdale County Alabama at the Eliza Coffee Memorial Hospital in Florence, Alabama.

Married

1st **Jenny Arnold** of Killen, Lauderdale County, Alabama. Divorced.

Children:

> **Constance Michelle Gray** born September 18, 1989. Constance is attending the University of South Alabama in Mobile, Alabama, where she will soon be a junior.

2nd On August 2nd, 2003 **Jennifer Ann Coonce Jones Edgar** at the Brookside Chapel in Mobile, Mobile County, Alabama. Jennifer is the daughter of Jean and Chris Coonce. Jennifer graduated from Satsuma High School in Satsuma, Alabama.

Jennifer had two children when she married Michael.

Jessica Brook Jones was born on June 2, 1994 to Jennifer and John Jones. Jessica is in the 10th grade at Mary G. Montgomery High School in Semmes, Alabama. She is a member of the Marching Vikings Flag corps. Following in her big sister Constance's footsteps.

Joanna Nicole Edgar was born on May 15, 1997 to Jennifer and Johnny Edgar. Joanna attends Semmes Middle School and is in the 8th grade. She is a member of the Bulldogs Concert band.

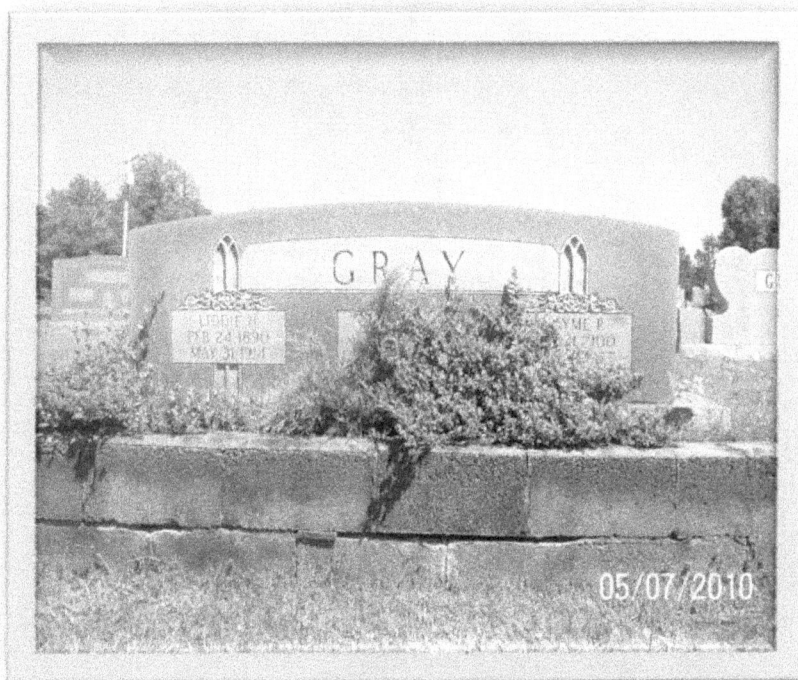

Grave marker of **Gus Gray** and his two wives, North Carolina Cemetery near Killen, Alabama.

MAYME R.
OCT. 21, 1900
AUG. 17, 1977

05/07/2010

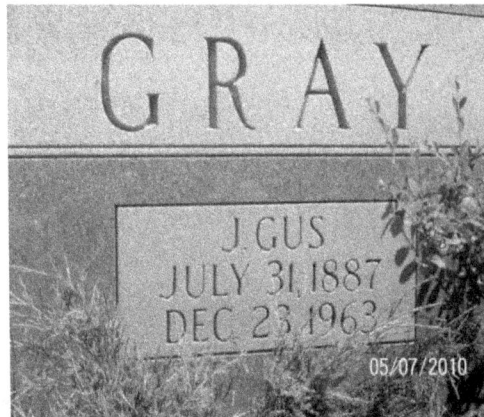

GRAY

J. GUS
JULY 31, 1887
DEC. 23, 1963

05/07/2010

LIDDIE H.
FEB. 24, 1890
MAY 31, 1914

05/07/2010

Chapter 16

James Gus Gray - Judith Ann McMurtrey Pedigree

James Gus Gray's Pedigree.

John Gray born January 26, 1820 in Tennessee, died October 20, 1864 in Greenhill, Lauderdale County, Alabama. Buried in the Wright cemetery Greenhill, Alabama.

Married **Bertha Wright** 1826-1885 on December 7, 1841.

Residence 1850 Division 2 East of the Military Road, Lauderdale County, Alabama.

Children:

> Mary Katharyn Gray 1842-
> Eliza Jane Gray 1843-1928
> James Warren Gray 1846-1889
> Bethany Elizabeth Gray 1848-1919
> John Dixon Gray 1849-1924
> Ephraim Newton Gray 1851-1919
> Banjamin Gilbert Gray 1853-1918
> Zelphia Ann Gray 1854-1936
> **James Minton Gray 1856-1898**
> William Henry Gray 1859-1939
> Rebecca Melvina Gray 1862-1932

James Minton Gray born December 15, 1856 in Lauderdale County, Alabama, died April 18, 1898 in Lauderdale County, Alabama. Buried in the North Carolina church cemetery near Greenhill, Alabama.

Married **Judith Ann McMurtrey** 1856-1942.

Residence 1880 Lauderdale County, Alabama.

Children:

> Robert Lee Gray
> C. Price Gray 1879-1939
> Mary Pernecia Gray 1884-1957
> **James Gus Gray 1887-1963**
> Adellia Ethel Gray 1890-1986
> Lucy Alice Gray 1893-1772
> Martha Melvina Gray 1895-

Judith Ann McMurtrey's Pedigree.

There was mention of McMurtrey ties by marriage with both the Rogers and Gray families so I thought the McMurtrey pedigree would be interesting.

William McMurtrey born 1755 in Atrim County, Ireland, died March 7, 1808 in Abbeville , Laurens County, South Carolina.

Emigrated December 20, 1772. Arrived Charles Town, South Carolina on board the Lord Dunlance.

Occupation Minister of the Covenanter Reform Presbyterian Church.

Married

Mary Puckett 1760-. Died in Laurens County, South Carolina.

Children:

> William C. McMurtrey 1782-1865
> **Matthew McMurtrey 1783-1863**
> Jenny McMurtrey 1784-
> Susanna M. McMurtrey 1786-
> Elizabeth McMurtrey 1788-1844
> Alexander Campbell McMurtrey 1791-1849

Matthew McMurtrey born 1783 in Laurens County, South Carolina, died September 3, 1863 in Lauderdale County, Alabama.

Married 1st **Ruth McDonald** 1790-1827.

Children:

1. William D. McMurtrey 1809-
2. Elizabeth McMurtrey 1810-
3. John McMurtrey 1814-1895. *Born November 2, 1814 died November 19, 1895. Married October 31, 1839* **Margaret Stutts** *1821-1887. Child* **Richard Bough (Bunn) McMurtrey** *born June 11, 1858 died May 27, 1939.* **Cecil McMurtrey's** *linage.*
4. Rachael McMurtrey 1816-
5. Lydia Ann McMurtrey 1818-

Married 2nd **Julia Clemons** in 1828.

Children:

John Matthew McMurtrey 1828-1862
Emaline McMurtrey 1833-1900
Rebecca McMurtrey 1835-1913
Curtis M. McMurtrey 1840-
Jessie McMurtrey 1841-1863

John Matthew McMurtrey born 1828 in Lauderdale County, Alabama, died July 13, 1862 in Murfreesboro, Tennessee.

Military:

He went to the battle of Murfreesboro and was never heard from again.

Married **Sarah Catherine Swinney**.

Children:

    Julia Ann McMurtrey

Julia Ann McMurtrey born July 24, 1856 in Lauderdale County, Alabama, died April 24, 1942 in Lauderdale County, Alabama. Buried in the North Carolina church cemetery near Greenhill, Alabama.

Married **James Minton Gray** 1856-1898. Seven children.

Residence 1880 Lauderdale County, Alabama.

Residence 1900 Greenhill, Lauderdale County, Alabama.

There are several McMurtreys buried in the North Carolina Church Cemetery between Greenhill and Killen, Alabama.

Chapter 17

Final Conclusion

Additional Information

I had chased all leads that I had to conclusion at this point and could think of no way to chase them any further. This was the beginning of February 2010.

I was visiting with Jerry Mitchell, the Mayor of Killen and an old friend and business acquaintance from the Reynolds Metals Company and later Wise Alloys in Muscle Shoals, Alabama, in late February to discuss a possible book signing for *One Family's Journey Through Time* at the Killen Library. Jerry Mitchell most graciously agreed and said that the Friends of the Killen Library would be most happy to host such an event.

During our conversation, Jerry mentioned that a play had been written about the 1884 trial of Frank James in Huntsville, Alabama regarding the Muscle Shoals payroll robbery in 1881. The play needed a slight revision to include the happenings in the Killen area before, during and after this robbery. The Killen Founder's Day committee was interested in producing this play during Founder's Day this year but could not get any interest stirred up locally to tackle the project of rewriting the play.

I immediately volunteered to run it by our Jackson County Advanced Writers' Group to see if they were willing to tackle this as a summer fun project. Jerry agreed to get me a copy of the play and he said that local historian and author Ronald Pettus had details of about the happenings that needed to be included in the play.

It took Jerry longer than anticipated to get a copy of the play for us and I met with Ronald Pettus in Athens, Alabama to get the required information from him. Ronald was quite generous with his information. He has extensive information archived about all the local happenings and facets of the trial which he shared with me. He just let me borrow the entire file! There is enough information in this portion of his archives for one to write a complete book!

I scanned a good portion of Ronald's material into my computer and printed copies for our writers' group to review. Jerry was able to send me the play by overnight delivery and it arrived the day of our meeting. After reviewing everything, the writers' group became most excited about this prospect for a fun summer project and accepted the challenge!

While reviewing Ronald Pettus' information, I noticed that one of the witnesses at the Frank James trial was one Alfred G. Hill of the Atlas community. I ran a quick and dirty internet search for information on him and found that his full name was Alfred Green Hill. This implication did not fully register at first but as I usually do while facing a perplexing problem, I kept mulling over it in my sleep. I awoke one morning with the thought in my mind–Alfred Green Hill–Green Hill–is there any connection with him and the town of Greenhill? It turned out that there was but the town was supposedly named after his uncle, Green Berry Hill!

According to the previously referenced information from Clara Rogers Clemons and U.S. census records, Joshua James and Esther Hicks James' oldest daughter, Sarah C. James, was born in 1830. Sarah C. James married Alfred Green Hill after his wife Lydia Harnell (Harrison?) died sometime in 1873. Joshua James and Esther Hicks James were also living in Atlas until their deaths in 1881 which is near where Alfred Green Hill was living at that time. The 1870 U.S. Census also lists Sarah C. James at age 43 living with her parents at that time.

Another member of the Joshua James household in 1870 was listed as **Morgan Matthews** age 9 who played a part in the earlier section of this saga as living as an orphan with William Joshua Rogers for a while in Giles County, Tennessee.

This would mean that Sarah C. James and Alfred Green Hill were husband and wife during the time leading up to the April 11, 1881 Muscle Shoals payroll robbery. According to The Huntsville Historical Review Vol 2, April 1972, Number 2, page12, by Leland R. Johnson and part of Ronald Pettus' archives, Alfred G. Hill also testified at Frank James' trial in Huntsville, Alabama in April 1884, that three men stayed at his house north of the canal before the robbery and made inquiry about the date the canal employees were paid. Neither he nor two other witnesses, Thomas Peden and Hugh Riley, bartender at Peden's saloon, could do more than say that Frank James resembled one of the men.

It is documented in the next section that Frank and Jesse James had a long-standing habit of visiting with relatives and friends at various times during their travels.

Although this is circumstantial evidence at best, I consider it to be the smoking gun that ties in the family of Joshua and Esther Hicks James directly with Frank and Jesse James. This is the link I had been searching for in my research.

What are the chances of Frank and Jesse James knocking on a total stranger's door asking to spend the night and end up staying at the home of someone whose maiden name was James? Not likely!

Part III

The Beginning of the End for the James Gang

Muscle Shoals Alabama Payroll Robbery

April 11, 1861

Chapter 18

Frank and Jesse James in Alabama Visiting with Relatives and Friends

It is well documented, as well as relayed by myths and legends, that over the years Frank and Jesse James had a habit of visiting with friends and relatives in Alabama.

There are such stories that I have tried to investigate earlier in this work and those to be detailed in this chapter. There is also a family in Jackson County, Alabama that claims being related to the James' family and the recipient of their visits. I have not had the opportunity to discuss this with any of them but I hope to in the near future. All of these claims may in fact have merit as the James family was large and very prolific. I am sure that they are scattered all the way from Wales to the far corners of America.

While there is a lot of information published about the James brothers outlaw years and much of it agrees in principal about the major events of this time in their lives, not all but some of it is different enough to conflict the timeline of the events and details. The information in the archives of Ronald Pettus is no different.

This is because the endless, deep, fathomless and notorious black bog of time has gobbled up most of the information that was available at one time but no more. This bog never gives up much meaningful information once it has gobbled it up.

That is why all of the references tell pretty much the same story but differ only in details and writing style. Everyone who writes about the activities of the James Gang is hashing and rehashing the same basic information and adding what details they feel are important to their story.

I will try to offer the major scenarios and differences as follows:

Visiting With Relatives and Friends

Montgomery Advertiser July 25, 1993–there were several articles about the activities of Frank and Jesse James in this issue.

An Article by Nick Lackeos, staff writer–Nick interviewed several people for this article and some of their accounts are listed as follows:

As a boy, **Gene Armstrong** heard his grandmother, who lived in Greenville, talk of Jesse visiting that area of the state.

"I heard he came to Greenville and stayed with two Alabama outlaws whose last names were Hipp and Kelley," said Mr. Armstrong, a collector of vintage guns and an expert in Wild West gunmen, who had an ancestor killed by **Hipp** and **Kelly**. "Frank (Jesse's brother) and Jesse used to hang out with Hipp and Kelly. And then they would drift up to Florence."

Nick Lackeos further quotes **Annie Crenshaw** of Wetumpka. She said she had a friend whose grandmother lived in Lowndes County in the late 1800s and remembers Jesse visiting when she was a small child.

"My friend lived in Fort Deposit, and she is the descendant of the James family," said Ms. Crenshaw, adding the woman's maiden name was also James. "Her grandmother used to remember them, Jesse and his men coming to their house."

She remembered there would be loud noise at night. There would be horses and riders, and the children would be told to go up to the loft. The riders would get food and horses and leave.

Nick Lackeos also quotes **Alice Lee**, 82 of Mount Willing in Lowndes County who also heard folk talk of Jesse James coming to the rural community.

"I always heard that he spent a month in Lowndes County about a half mile from my house," said Miss Lee, a member of the Lowndes County Historical and Genealogical Society.

"The place where Jesse James stayed was back toward Hayneville from the (Bill) Jones store. We think that may be the reason he came here was that these people he stayed with were relatives. But they would never admit it."

"Their last name was Garrett. **Miss Belle Garrett** – it was her parents that he stayed with. She later married a Scarborough."

Nick Lackeos also references comments made by **Mr. Jamie Wallace**, president of the Selma and Dallas Chamber of Commerce who researched the James brothers' travels when he was a student at the University of Alabama in the 1950s.

Some of Mr. Wallace's comments were about the attractiveness of Alabama for the James brothers.

"One of the draws Alabama had for the James brothers was their close, boyhood friend, **John Green Norris**, who settled in Selma after the Civil War," Mr. Wallace said.

"Norris and Frank joined the Confederate Army together early in the Civil War when Jesse was too young to go, about age 15."

"Frank rode with bands of Confederate guerrillas in Missouri, including Quantrill's Raiders, led by William Quantrill," said Bob Bradley, head of special collections at the Alabama Department of Archives and History.

"Later in the war in 1864 at age 17, Jesse joined Frank in another band of guerrillas led by "Bloody Bill" Anderson, Mr. Bradley said. Riding with this group, Jesse learned to kill, he said of combat with Union soldiers.

Mr. Bradley said in a later part of this article that Jesse and Frank lived in Jackson County, Tennessee, for several years, beginning about 1877, with their wives and children. Jesse Woodson James, who was called "Dingus" by his friends, used the alias of John Davis "Dave" Howard and his brother, Alexander Franklin James, went by B. J. Woodson. (*I hadn't heard of the James brothers living in Jackson, Tennessee before.*)

"Also in the James brothers' favor was public sentiment, at least in the South," Mr. Wallace said. Many Southerners were bitter about the Civil War and saw the James Gang as striking a blow of revenge by hitting Union backed banks and the trains of Northern based railroads.

Chapter 19

James Boys Visit Selma Alabama

There is another article in the **July 25, 1993 issue of the Montgomery Advertiser** that was about a visit or possible visits by Frank and Jesse James to Selma, Alabama and it was also written by Nick Lackeos. He interview **Mr. Jamie Wallace**, president of the Selma and Dallas Chamber of Commerce in depth for this article.

Mr. Lackeos starts this article by stating, "Whenever Jesse James rode deep into Alabama, it was sure that he would spend a week or so in Selma."

"This is where he stayed when he came to Selma, right here on Water Avenue at the St. James Hotel."

"I always heard that Jesse made more than one visit here (Selma) and he liked to gamble and visit the red-light district," which was part of Water Avenue (also called Water Street) in the late 19th century" Mr. Wallace said.

"The St. James was an upscale hotel–apparently pretty ornate," Mr. Wallace said.

"The St. James was a respectable hotel, but farther down the street in less expensive hotels passengers from docked riverboats and trains that stopped at the depot several blocks away could find female companions for the evening," he said.

"Jesse and Frank registered at the St. James under the alias of Williams. And they didn't stay in the same room. They stayed in separate rooms so that if one got captured, the other one could break him out of jail," Mr. Williams further added.

"While in Selma they visited their boyhood friend, John Green Norris, who may have also been a cousin. Norris grew up with Jesse and Frank, and they lived in the same household back in Missouri," Mr. Wallace added.

"Jesse and Frank came here to visit Norris but they didn't stay with him at his home because they didn't want to cause the Norris family any trouble," said Mr. Wallace, adding that it is said that they never robbed in the Selma area out of respect for their friend.

"After having supper at the Norris house, the James brothers would return to their hotel where they played billiards in the game room with James Dedham, the St. James manager, who described them as perfect gentlemen," Mr. Wallace said. "Jesse also sat in on saloon card games and spent time in the Water Avenue red-light district," he said.

From W. Stanley Hoole, THE JAMES BOYS RODE SOUTH, FRANK AND JESSE JAMES AND THEIR COMRADES IN CRIME, page 19-20, 1955, Privately printed for the Author in Tuscaloosa, Alabama

Mr. W. Stanley Hoole offers more information as to the relationship between Frank and Jesse James and John Green Norris.

In Clay County, Missouri the farm owned by the James' family in the middle of the last century adjoined that belonging to one **Frank Silas Norris** and his wife, Sarah, both families having migrated from the same section of Kentucky in the '40s and '50s. Like their next door neighbors, the Norrises had two children: a daughter whose name has somehow been lost down through the years, and a son, John Green Norris, who grew up a playmate of Frank and Jesse James, romping the rolling hills with them and swimming in the creek or working side by side in the broad family fields of corn and wheat.

When the war for Southern Independence broke out, John Green Norris – as did his nineteen-year-old friend, Alexander Franklin James – enlisted in the Confederate Army. Little Jesse, a lad of but fourteen or fifteen, remained at home.

Author's note – What does all of this that supposedly happened in South Alabama have to do with the James boys activity in North Alabama? It illustrates their pattern of visiting with friends and relatives anywhere. They were a cautious pair and the pattern of these visits illustrates this.

Chapter 20

Jesse James and Family Arrive in the Nashville Area

From the archives of Ronald Pettus - **Jesse James-Rabbit Man of Humphreys County** by Raymond W. Thorp, page 1 and 2, May 1965 Frontier Times, courtesy Western Publications.

On a sunny spring day in 1878, a brand new wagon uncovered, wended its way down the long hill which overlooks the town of Waverly, Tennessee. The outfit was drawn by a pair of beautiful bay mares, and inside the wagon was a man, a woman and two small children – a girl and a boy.

The driver was young in appearance, with a three day stubble of beard on his face, which, with the high cheek-bones, gave him a somewhat sinister look. He was clothed in workaday clothing of the time and place – that of a Tennessee farmer. The woman beside him on the seat was very comely, as she smiled as she looked down at the prattling children at her feet, behind the dashboard of the Studebaker rig.

"Do you think Ma would like this move?" she asked, looking at her companion. He had been busy watching the trees alongside the roadside, but now he looked at her, and his eyes softened as his sharp features relaxed a trifle. "It is the best we can do," he replied, "and we'll be better off with a little rest."

"Ma don't like any move I make," he added. "You know that, hon. But she knows the Northfield men are still hanging around. I think we'll be all right here."

W. A. McCutcheon, the owner of the Nolan House, the only hostelry in Waverly, came outside when the rig stopped outside his place.

"How's chances for me and my family to put up with you for a few days?" the stranger asked him. Immediately a crowd had gathered admiring the splendid team of horses. The boy and girl stood up now, but holding onto their mother's dress as if fearful of the rough men of Tennessee.

McCutcheon stepped into the street and looked at the foursome. "Strangers in the Big Bottom?" he asked stroking one of the mares.

"Yes, but not for long. We mean to settle here. I already have a place picked out," replied the stranger.

The hotel man quickly came to life, held up his arms and deposited the woman and children on the ground. "Go inside and tell my wife to show you where to wash off that hill dust," he told her, and then to the driver, "Drive down that alleyway and we'll put up the team in my stable."

He climbed upon the seat, and the outfit moved away, with the crowd still gaping. After a Negro boy had put up the team, the stranger signed the register for himself and family: **J. D. Howard, Louisville, Kentucky**.

The next day Howard leased for a year the **W. N. Link** farm a few miles from Box Station, later known as Denver, and the following Saturday two carloads of household goods arrived. Henry Harris, the station agent, upon being told by Howard that he was temporarily out of funds, quickly defrayed the charges with true southern generosity. Harris had looked over the goods carefully, and knew they were the best that money could buy.

Frank James' arrival to the Nashville, Tennessee area is not documented as well but in Frank's trial in Huntsville, Alabama, as reported in an article in **The Nashville Tennessean Magazine**, February 15, 1971 from testimony by Jonas Taylor, he met Ben Woodson in Nashville in 1878. They were introduced by Berry Cheatham. He said Woodson lived on the **Drake** place on White's Creek and later on the **Smith** place and again nearer town.

Jesse James and his family had arrived in the Nashville, Tennessee area where they would spend the next few years of their life and fit in quite well into the Waverly community. Who knows, if it had not been for the Lock Six payroll robbery in Muscle Shoals, Alabama and its aftermath, perhaps he and Frank James could have lived out their lives in peace in the Nashville area.

The balance of the booklet is full of details given to the author Raymond W. Thorp by the sheriff of Humphreys County, Tennessee, **J. P. (Jim) White**. Jim White witnessed firsthand many of the details in this booklet and participated in some of them. It deals with how Jesse James and his family settled into the area, their activities socially in the community, how Frank James as Mr. J. P. Woodson interacted and the flight from the Nashville area back to Missouri. This is probably the most exact account of any part of this notorious outlaw's life.

Chapter 21

Planning of Robbery

There are several different accounts about the planning of this robbery.

In the July 25, 1993 issue of the Montgomery Advertiser , Mr. Nick Lackeos quotes information from Mr. Jamie Wallace pinpointing the location of the James brothers before the Muscle Shoals Alabama Lock Six robbery as follows:

Although it is believed the James brothers made many trips to Selma for visits, published statements from Norris place the James brothers in Selma in March of 1881, the month of the robbery of an Army paymaster in Florence. Mr. Wallace said he interviewed Norris' son, **Frank Silas Norris II** in 1955, then a retired Southern Railway engineer who was living in Selma on Alabama Avenue.

Mr. Wallace conducted the interview while researching the James brothers visit to the state as a student at the University of Alabama in the 1950s.

"The Norris I talked to was the son of the man that Jesse and Frank visited," he said, "And he showed me some stiff shirt cuffs that Jesse had autographed and given to his father."

Mr. Norris also showed Mr. Wallace a telegram that was yellowed with age. It was sent collect to the Norris family from Jesse's widow from Kansas City, Missouri on November 5, 1903 giving Frank's address, 4229 Leclede in St. Louis. He also showed Mr. Wallace an autographed photograph of Jesse that had been made in New Orleans.

"He's dead now," said Mr. Wallace of the Norris that he interviewed. He doesn't know what happened to the James artifacts but he believes they were passed down to other members of the Norris family.

Author's note: The James brothers couldn't have done much planning for the Lock Six robbery if they were in Selma at the time.

From **W. Stanley Hoole, THE JAMES BOYS RODE SOUTH, FRANK AND JESSE JAMES AND THEIR COMRADES IN CRIME, excerpts from pages 35, 37, 1955. Privately printed for the author in Tuscaloosa, Alabama.**

From testimony at Frank James April 1884 trial in Huntsville, Alabama, **James Andrew Liddil**, known to banditry history as Dick Liddil, onetime member of the James outfit, who had been brought all the way from his Kansas City, Missouri jail cell by United States Marshal W. I. Overton to betray his former friend and comrade-in-crime.

Author's note: Although Dick Liddil's testimony was largely disregarded by the jury in the Frank James' trial, the time frame in this part of it matches the timing of the robbery.

"Frank, Jesse and "Wild Bill" Ryan had set off on March 6 toward the South, intending to arrange for a train robbery later in the spring, and mark out a line of retreat," he testified. Further adding, "Upon the James' advice, he (Liddil) had headed for Adairsville, Kentucky, just across the Tennessee border, forty miles due north of Nashville, to hide out in the home of his friend, George T. Hite and his sons, Robert Woodson Hite, alias "Ole Grimes," and Clarence Browler Hite, sometimes members of the James' gang and favorite first cousins of Frank and Jesse.

This part is interesting but not part of the planning of the Lock Six robbery at Muscle Shoals. Continuing with Dick Liddil's testimony.

(Incidentally Dick saw no need to mention a few minor details: Wood and Clarence Hite had taken active parts in the Glendale, Winston, and Blue Cut train robberies of 1879 and 1881; he, Liddil, had been accused of "carrying on" with Mrs. George T. Hite, vivacious, young stepmother of Wood and Clarence, and again, he, Liddil, had on December 4, 1881 put a bullet neatly through Wood Hite's head "two inches above the right eye" because "Old Grimes" had accused him of snitching more than was his honest share of the proceeds of the Blue Cut stick-up. Poor memory, that's all. . .)

This part is taken from **Lauderdale County Alabama, Cops and Robbers - (Mostly Robbers), Frank and Jesse James Robbery in 1881, (page 1). Compiled April 2004, by Lee Freeman.**

From the Tuscumbia, Alabama, *North Alabamian and Times*, Friday March 18, 1881, p. 3.

One of them is a heavy set, broad faced, sandy haired man about 35 years old, with a hare lip, and about 5 feet 9 inches high, and rode a dark bay horse with a bald face. Number two is a thin visaged, consumptive looking fellow, about 38 years old with a light mustache and chin whiskers, about 5 feet 10, and rode a sorrel horse with all white feet. Number three is about 5 feet 10, with dark brown whiskers, weighs about 175 pounds and rode a dappled grey horse or mare with bald face. He looked to be about 28 years old, went by the name of Capt. Jack and talked like he might be an Irishman.

All three of them had been hanging around the canal for a week or two, one of them claiming to be a fruit tree peddler and the other two hinting that they were Revenue officers.

Author's note - This would have given them ample time to case out the canal.

From the testimony of Alfred Green Hill at Frank James' 1884 trial in Huntsville, Alabama:

Alfred Green Hill testified at the Frank James April 1884 trial in Huntsville, Alabama that according to **The Huntsville Historical Review** Vol 2, April 1972, Number 2 page12 by Leland R. Johnson and part of Ronald Pettus' Archives, that three men stayed at his house north of the canal before the robbery and made inquiry about the date the canal employees were paid. Neither he nor another witness Hugh Riley, bartender at Peden's saloon, could do more than say that Frank James resembled one of the men.

Testimony of **Thomas Peden** at the 1884 trial of Frank James in Huntsville, Alabama.

There were three references to the testimony of Thomas Peden at the trial.

1. **The Huntsville Historical Review,** Vol 2, April 1972 page 10 and 11, "The James Gang in Huntsville" by Leland R. Johnson.

2. Article by Max York in **The Nashville Tennessean Magazine**, February 28, 1971.

3. **"Jesse James, The Last Rebel Of The Civil War**," by T. J. Stiles, Knopf 2002.

All of these references cover pretty much the same information, each more detailed than the other in certain areas. I will quote from Max York as he covers more details of what happened at Peden's Saloon the day of the Lock Six robbery.

The government's first witness was **Thomas Peden** –"Old Man Peden, a well to do countryman," who kept a saloon near the works at Muscle Shoals.

Peden testified that on March 11, 1881, three men came into his saloon and hitched their horses under a shade tree. One man had black whiskers and was tolerably well dressed. The other two were lighter. The men had a couple of drinks and two of them walked out. The third settled the bill.

Peden sat on a lumber pile with one of the men for half an hour, talking. The man wanted to talk about the canal. They also talked politics. The man also wanted to know how the Negroes were doing. Had slaves been hard to manage?

After a while the men ate cheese and crackers and rode off to the east. Two of the riders went out first. The third followed 100 to 130 yards behind on a sorrel **with a peculiar lump on its back.**

Author's note: Their reconnaissance done and all of the information gathered that they could get, the three men were now ready to commit the robbery.

The next day Peden heard about the robbery.

In his opinion, Frank James was one of these three men. However, on cross-examination, he was not so sure.

Walker (Frank James' Chief Defense Attorney) had James put on a slouch hat, the kind the three men were wearing that day, and parade back and forth in front of the witness. After that, Peden said he couldn't swear that James was the man.

"Mr. James," Peden said, "If you did the robbery, you ought to be punished. I'd say your nose and forehead look like the man, but I can't say you are the man."

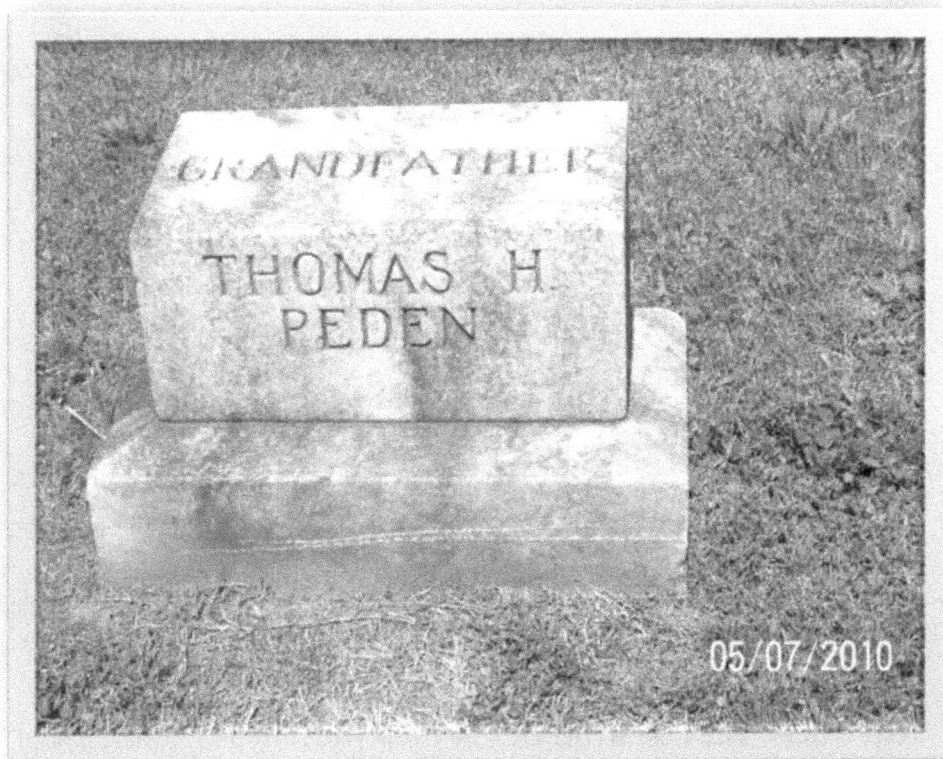

Grave marker of **Thomas H. Peden**, Killen Cemetery, Killen, Alabama.

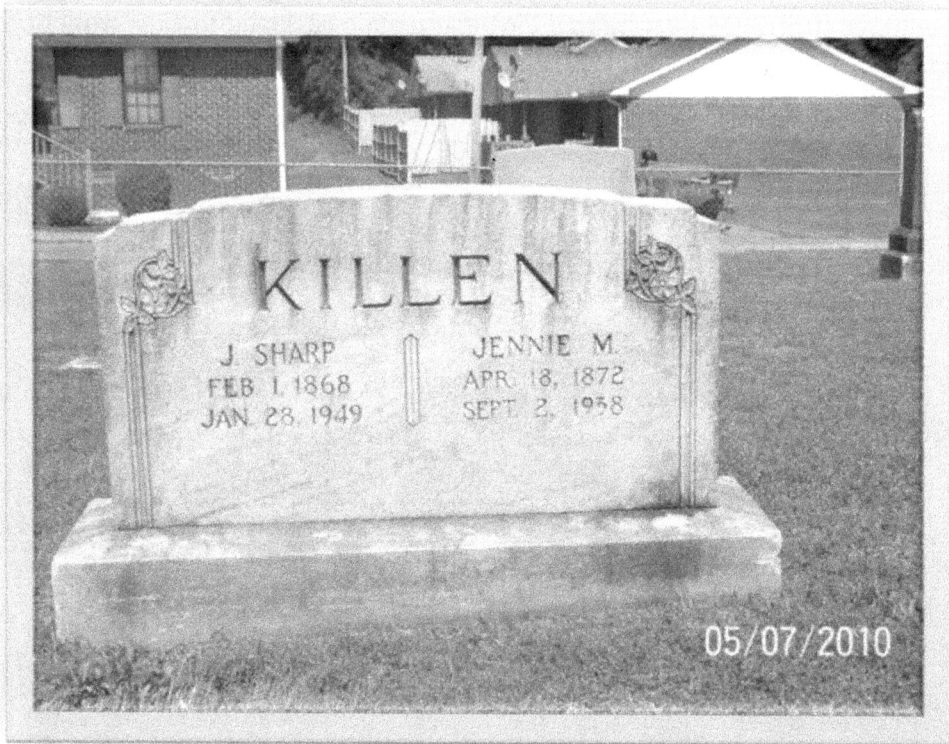

Grave marker of **J. Sharp Killen** and his wife **Jennie M. Peden Killen**. Jennie was the daughter of **Thomas H. Peden**. Killen Cemetery, Killen, Alabama. Thomas Peden's grave is nearby.

From "**Jesse James, The Last Rebel Of The Civil War**," by T. J. Stiles, Knopf 2002.

Author's Note: This is the only reference to the planning stages of the robbery that indicated that Frank James was indeed not part of this robbery but another man was the third robber.

Having disposed of these distractions, Jesse resumed his relentless cascade of holdups. In early 1881, he set out with Ryan and another man, probably Wood (*"Old Grimes")* Hite (*who lived in Adairsville, near Russellville, Logan County, Kentucky. This was supposedly the headquarters of the James Gang at that time, the Hite farm*).

He (Jesse) had discovered a particularly inviting target: a remote army engineering crew working on the Muscle Shoals canal in northern Alabama. At ten o'clock on March 11, 1881, Jesse led his two followers to Thomas H. Peden's saloon, just 100 yards from the canal. The innkeepers recollections were riddled with inaccuracies, but he did notice that one man had something wrong with a finger **(From The James-Younger Gang: Outlaws, an internet source. Jesse had lost the 1st joint of his third finger on his left hand.)** This fellow was "very correct & intelligent in conversation, quick spoken, and to all appearances, the leader of the crowd," Peden said. "He talked politics most of the time, remarking that he was well acquainted with Secretaries Windom & Lincoln." (This was a reference to William Windom and Robert Todd Lincoln, the newly designated heads of the Treasury and War Departments, respectively.) Jesse seemed particularly interested in the incoming president, James A. Garfield. He also inquired in detail about whether "the Negroes in slavery" had been harder to "manage" than they were now.

Chapter 22

Execution of Robbery

There are several versions of the robbery, all agree in principal but differ somewhat in the details. I will quote from W. Stanley Hoole. His version seems to be very complete.

W. Stanley Hoole, THE JAMES' BOYS RODE SOUTH, FRANK AND JESSE JAMES AND THEIR COMRADES IN CRIME, page 25-28, 1955. Privately printed for the author in Tuscaloosa, Alabama.

Alexander G. Smith, United States Army Paymaster, strolled nonchalantly out of the Campbell and Coat banking company, Florence, Alabama and slung a heavy saddlebag over his horse's back. Glancing quickly at his gold watch, he swung into his saddle and slowly galloped down the muddy street toward the Engineer's Camp at Bluewater on the Tennessee River a few miles upstream from Florence toward Rogersville. It was four o'clock on Friday afternoon March 11, 1881.

A few minutes later, as he jogged unhurriedly along the tow-path that paralleled the Muscle Shoals Canal, a scant two miles from Florence, three masked horsemen with pistols drawn sprang out of the brush, disarmed him, grabbed the saddlebag, and tied his hands behind his back. From his pocket they took $221 and his watch. But, after a brief whispered conference, they returned the timepiece and $21. Then, cautiously they drove their victim at gunpoint through the dense forest, generally toward the direction of the Tennessee border.

In these few moments $5,200 had changed hands-$500 in gold, and $4,500 in fifties, twenties, and smaller currency in the saddlebag and $200 from paymaster Smith's purse.

And in those few moments the world's most notorious desperados – robbers of banks, trains and express cars North and West – had successfully accomplished their only mission in banditry in the deep south. Even now, seventy-five years later, their names are known to every school child: the fabulous Frank and Jesse James of Missouri. Their partner in crime at Muscle Shoals was **"Wild Bill" Ryan**, alias Tom Hill, a bold fearless braggart whose liking for liquor made him sometimes dangerously loose-tongued.

Silently, the four horsemen wove their way through the wild, deserted forest, a wilderness unbroken save the work camps of the United States Engineers at intervals of several miles along the Muscle Shoals Canal. At dusk, the robbers removed their masks and became familiarly talkative. They told Paymaster Smith that they were Texans, that they had been lurking in the neighborhood, plotting the payroll robbery for more than a week. They bragged that they were not strangers to the region, having passed through the canal zone more than once on missions into South Alabama. (Smith later noted that they "understood the country pretty well") One of the men, the noisy one, loudly declared that they should shoot the paymaster, now that he had "brought" them all this money. But the second, obviously the leader, angrily replied that they were not killers and that he alone, if necessary, would permit no personal harm to the captive.

As they rode on hour after hour, pass Bull's Mill and Center Star and into the darkness of the forest, the bandits probed Paymaster Smith with questions and nervously bantered him with small talk. This time they told him they were Tennessee farmers – good ones, too. (Smith later recalled that they were "dressed the part.") And when the paymaster replied to their question, "Who the devil are you, anyhow?" One of the robbers joked, "Smith, eh? Well, I'm Smith, too-I am yours truly Henry Smith!" His companions joined heartily in the laughter.

In constant dread, Paymaster Smith but frightfully marvel about the good-natured nonchalance of the three desperados. One of the men, the oldest, seemed almost a preacher, at times quoting bits from Shakespeare or the Bible. The second was a loud-mouthed braggart and the third, the youngest man, was talkative to be true, but sharp eyed and ever alert.

Four hours and twenty miles after the hold-up the men stopped in a dense, deeply secluded spot. The bandits unsaddled, squatted on the ground, and "Henry Smith" carefully divided the $5,200 equally among his partners and himself. Then they untied their victim's arms and remounted their horses. As they sped away into the darkness, one of the men threw the unfortunate paymaster an overcoat, shouting, "Pass the night comfortably, Mr. Smith."

The bewildered official wandered all night through the thick, black, unfamiliar forest. Towards dawn a terrific thunderstorm struck the area, blinding the lost man and chilling him to the bone. Not until Saturday noon did he stumble into Bluewater camp, weary and ill. His companions eagerly told him of the several searching parties which had been out since yesterday's sunset, combing the woods along the canal between the camp and Florence. Only with the coming of the storm had they called off the hunt and giving him up for dead, believing him murdered. . .

From an undated article in the Times Daily in Florence, an article by Dennis Sherer tells a little different story. Dennis quotes **Jesse Clopton James**, a Florence native and a fourth cousin to the famous outlaw duo. Jesse Clopton James researched the James Gang's robbery of the paymaster of the Muscle Shoals Canal project.

According to the present day James, who lives in Fountain Valley, California, after dividing the money, "Wild Bill" then went north, Frank and Jesse went south and Smith was left in the woods.

He also states that Frank and Jesse spent the night at the home of their second cousin, **Elias James**, near Pogo in Franklin County (Alabama, Tennessee? There is one in both states) and eventually made their way to their home near Nashville, Tennessee, about two days later.

Chapter 23

The Aftermath and the Flight Back to Missouri

From **The Huntsville Historical Review Vol 2, April 1972 Number 2, pages 5-7**, by Leland R. Johnson.

A well dressed stranger rode into White Creek, a village near Nashville, Tennessee, entered a saloon and ordered raw oysters and raw whiskey with predictable results – he got drunk, flourished a pistol, and it took several strong men to disarm him. A search of the stranger, who told them his name was "Tom Hill," revealed that he was carrying almost $1500 in gold coin. He was turned over to the Nashville police, and the large sum of cash in his possession brought him under suspicion in the Muscle Shoals robbery. Alexander G. Smith was summoned to Nashville, where he identified Hill as one of the men who had robbed him. The cash in the possession of Hill was attached by Nashville authorities and eventually returned to the United States government. Nashville police wired a description of the man to law enforcement officials around the country and word came back from Missouri that "Tom Hill" was none other that than "William Ryan," alias Jack Ryan, known by some as "Whiskey Head" Ryan, a member of the notorious Jesse James Gang.

It was eventually discovered that Jesse and Frank James had lived with their families in homes in and around Nashville from about 1875 until the capture of Ryan in 1881. Except for a fondness for fast horses, which they rode in local fairs, they passed as respectable citizens, Jesse under the name of J. D. "Tom" Howard and Frank as B. J. "Ben" Woodson. Neither attracted much attention at the time, although their long absences from home were later recalled by those who had long been acquainted with them. The robbery of the Engineers at Muscle Shoals and the subsequent capture of "Whiskey Head" Ryan apparently forced them to give up their hideout in Nashville, for those events had brought the United States Marshals into the manhunt. The two brothers evidently returned to Missouri, a heavy reward was placed on their heads. Jesse James, while living under his Howard alias in St. Joseph, Missouri, was shot by Robert Ford on April 3, 1882. Not long thereafter Frank James surrendered himself to the governor of Missouri.

Meanwhile at the scene of the Muscle Shoals robbery in North Alabama, United States Marshal Lionel W. Day, and others, quietly gathered the evidence in the case at Huntsville. Affidavits were collected from Alexander Smith, Major King, and others and a warrant was issued against William Ryan, but the Justice Department chose to let Missouri officials handle Ryan, for proof was positive in the case pending against Ryan there. By October, 1882, enough evidence had been collected to convince a federal grand jury in Huntsville that the members of the James Gang were culprits. The jury brought back a blanket indictment.

From **The James Boys In The Valley**, by Henry Walker, Athens, November 1966, page 16-17.

While the prisoner in the Nashville jail – who for precautionary reasons sometimes called himself Tom Hill – was trying to construct a believable alibi for having nearly $1300 in gold and greenbacks on his person, a tall, thin man rode out of the gate of his farm a few miles north of Nashville, bound for the farm of Mr. Howard.

The horseman, whom his neighbors knew as B. J. Woodson, raised Poland China hogs, which he sold on the Nashville market. But he also grew corn and grain to feed them, and in this late March of 1881, with planting-time near on him, he needed some good mules. And this J. B. Howard , who like himself, had lived in this Tennessee region but four years, was supposed to have some young but workable stock for sale.

But when Woodson reached the Howard place, the price of mules never entered the conversation between the two stockmen.

"Jesse," Woodson told the blond, slimly built man who met him as he dismounted, "that damned Irishman of yours has done it now. He's been drunk over a week and busted into Earthman's place, shot it up and popped off his mouth. They've got him in the Nashville jail now, and if I know Bill Ryan, he'll tell 'em anything to save his own sorry hide."

The man called Jesse and who went by the name of Howard just blinked his eyes several times, a habit he'd had since boyhood.

"Frank, Bill's all right 'long as he's sober; he just got too much liquor in him. But I don't guess we can take a chance. You and Annie and the boy get ready, we got to get out of here. Maybe we'd better go on ahead and let them and Zee follow with the kids. I'll meet you on the road."

Thus ended for Jesse and Frank James the happiest years they had known since embarking on a crime career that was to make them world-infamous, enduring legends that are part of America's folk-lore.

Had they resisted the temptation to rob the government payroll at Muscle Shoals, less than a month before, they might have lived out their years in an uneasy kind of security in Middle Tennessee, well-thought of by their neighbors and, with their wives and children, ordinary members of an ordinary Southern community.

From "**Jesse James, The Last Rebel Of The Civil War**," by T. J. Stiles, Knopf 2002.

Muscle Shoals was the perfect robbery–but its aftermath was a disaster. On March 25, 1881, Ryan, passing under the name of Thomas Hill, departed from the Hite farm in Kentucky, a few miles north of Nashville, he decided to stop for a drink at a store on White's Creek turnpike. Before long he was drunk. Turning to **W. L. Earthman**, he roared in his distinctive Irish accent that "he was an outlaw against State, county and the Federal Government, and was now acting as a government detective." Unfortunately for Ryan, Earthman was *Justice* Earthman, of Davidson County. In short order, Earthman had Ryan under arrest. On patting him down, he found two revolvers and some $1400. Five days later, Smith walked into the Nashville jail to see the prisoner, and immediately recognized him as one of the Muscle Shoals bandits.

The day after Ryan's arrest was Saturday. Liddil was at Jesse James' house that afternoon. Since Jesse thought it best to stay inside so soon after a robbery, Liddil went into Nashville for him to collect money from the sale of some of Jesse's furniture. "I got an evening paper," Liddil recalled, "and saw from the description (of the arrested man) that it was Ryan. I went over and told Jesse and Frank." For the increasingly edgy Jesse, the capture must have conjured up the ghosts of **Hobbs Kerry**. Ryan too, was a non-bushwhacker recruit who had been caught because of his reckless behavior. In this case, however, the danger stemmed not only from the imprisoned bandit, but from the man who made the arrest. The two James brothers knew W. L. Earthman personally, having met him at a racetrack in 1879. It would not take him long to connect Ryan to the man he knew as J. D. Howard.

Both brothers decided to flee Nashville immediately. That same day they set out for the Hite farm with Liddil. Jesse sent Zee and the children to Donny Pence's home, in Nelson County, Kentucky, and Frank sent Annie and little Robert on to Kansas City by train.

From the before referenced **Jesse James, Rabbit Man of Humphreys County by Raymond W. Thorp, page 9 and 10.**

Author's note: The year and season of the flight to Missouri is in dispute with other published accounts. But this could have been the scenario as it played out.

When Howard disposed of his cattle in the fall, neighbors surmised that he was ready to leave Tennessee. However, when he paid up his lease for another full year, they settled back, confident that no one in his right mind would pay up a lease and then move out.

Old timers of Humphreys County have vouched for the fact that the winter of **1879-80** was a cold one. And in the middle of one of the coldest nights, six large wagons filled with household goods rolled through Waverly from Big Bottom, headed west. Twenty head of saddle horses followed, in turn followed by a covered wagon.

At the head of the caravan rode the Rabbit Man (Jesse James) on Red Fox and seemingly very untimid. He sat in his famous saddle with the big holsters that had excited comment, but the holsters were not empty now. From each of them peeped what appeared to be a wooden plow handle, actually the grip of huge Walker Colt's pistols.

A farmer boy who was out late watched the procession from among the trees into which he had ridden when he heard the wagon wheels approaching, and later told the sheriff, "Mr. Howard and his friend were pretty heavy with weapons. The Rabbit Man had two brand new Colt .45 pistols in his belt, and a Winchester rifle across his saddle. Mr. Woodson carried a double barreled shotgun and his regular pistols."

"The boy didn't tell me until the following week," said Sheriff White, "and maybe it was just as well."

Bringing up the rear-guard was B. J. Woodson, similarly armed and equipped and with keen eyes scanning the roadside. The last wagon was covered with canvas, with a hole in the rear, and he was talking through that hole. "Zee, I'll bet you will be glad to see Ma again," he said.

Mrs. Howard looked at him and replied, "Frank, that will be a joyful day. We had to watch the mail, you know, and she couldn't come to see us. But the hardest job of all was to try to hold Jesse down. It was bad on him and bad on me."

"Well, we're headin' for old Missouri now," Woodson told her.

It was three days before anyone learned that the Howards were missing. Then, when two men did ride that way, they found only a bare empty house, with chickens scratching in the yard. They caught and trussed the later, to take them home. But the Howards had left something besides chickens behind them. As the men rode away they saw under an old apple tree a double mound, with a large stone marker between them. It was the grave of the twins (born during their stay in the Nashville, Tennessee, area). The wagons were still rolling onward toward the west.

From "**Jesse James, The Last Rebel Of The Civil War**," by T. J. Stiles, Knopf 2002.

Author's note: There was some tension at the Hite farm while Frank, Jesse and Liddil were resting there after they fled Nashville. Three suspicious heavily armed men were seen riding by the house.

After the tension lifted, Liddil, Frank and Jesse joined Zee at the Pence home. She and the children went to Louisville with Clarence (from the Hite house) to catch a train back to Kearney (*Missouri*). Just before she took the cars, she reportedly raised some $70 by renting a horse and buggy and selling both to a pair of unsuspecting gentlemen. A week later Liddil and Jesse took the same route. The two men rode stolen horses all the way to the depot; indeed Jesse was a chronic and indiscriminate horse thief.

Frank lingered in Kentucky for another week before reluctantly departing for Missouri. His life had been upended overnight, and it left him depressed. "Try as we might to break off from our Bohemian life, something would always occur to drive us back," he reflected a year and a half after the escape from Nashville. "It was with a sense of despair that drove us away from our little home…and again became a wanderer." He blamed the reckless Ryan for his troubles, but he must have seen that the real cause was closer at hand. No matter how hard he worked nor what choices he made, his fate was lashed tight to his younger brother's impulsive decisions. What he could not know was how soon that it would end.

Chapter 24

Trial

The events of the trial of Frank James in Huntsville, Alabama in April of 1884 are well- documented by published accounts. All of them are different in the reporting of details and writing style.

Three of the references that I have chosen to review and extract excerpts from for this section are:

1. W. Stanley Hoole, THE JAMES BOYS RODE SOUTH, FRANK AND JESSE JAMES AND THEIR COMRADES IN CRIME, 52 pages, 1955, Privately printed for the author in Tuscaloosa, Alabama.

2. The Huntsville Historical Review Vol 2, April 1972 Number 2 pages 5-7, by Leland R. Johnson

3. Article by Max York in **The Nashville Tennessean Magazine**, February 28, 1971.

From **W. Stanley Hoole, THE JAMES BOYS RODE SOUTH, FRANK AND JESSE JAMES AND THEIR COMRADES IN CRIME, excerpts from pages 32-35, 1955. Privately printed for the author in Tuscaloosa, Alabama.**

But down deep in the Deep South, six hundred miles away, (*from Frank James' problems in Missouri*) there was yet an old score to be settled. Someone had to pay society for the $5,200 Muscle Shoals robbery. And since Jesse was dead and "Wild Bill" Ryan was already serving a twenty-five year sentence, Alabama authorities were sure that the notorious Frank James was their man. Thus, although freed in Missouri, he was refused bail by United States Judge Judy Krekel and in February, 1884, the unhappy gunman was hustled aboard a train and under guard taken to Huntsville, Alabama.

Again, interminable delays, while Frank languished day after day in the filthy, flea ridden Madison County jail. For men, women and children a curiosity behind bars, he spoke gently to those who questioned him, sensing that his notoriety had made him something akin to public property. Two months went by as his waking hours were increasingly filled with reading – Shakespeare he liked best of all – and with happy visits from Huntsville's old Confederates, men who, like himself had rallied 'round the Stars and Bars in those daring days of 1861.

Not until Thursday, April 17 did District Attorney L. W. Day read the indictment against Frank James before United Circuit Court and twenty-odd government witnesses from the Muscle Shoals vicinity file forth to testify in the humid, crowded courtroom. Yes, they had seen the "three mysterious horsemen" in 1881. . .yes they had, but they couldn't now be *too* sure. After all it had been three years ago, you know. Four witnesses strangely remembered the horses better than they did the riders, but even their descriptions, as the Huntsville *Democrat* reported, were "not altogether agreeing within."

One witness, Tom Peden the saloonkeeper from over at Canal Lock Three near Florence, amused everyone by requiring the sheriff to put a "slouch hat" on Frank and walk him about the courtroom, a feat the accused performed "with a firm, steady eye to and fro." Peden was confident he had seen the defendant somewhere; but, after all, lots of men could come into a saloon in three years – well, he couldn't be *too* sure.

Next Paymaster Smith, himself, was called to the stand. Dramatically, as if he were draining the role of every pleasurable drop, he told his story. The road between Florence and Bluewater Camp was at best a dangerous one – everyone knew that, he began. Besides, he had told Major King and Chief Engineer Gillette of the myriad risks involved in the poor lone man's carrying all that money over that dreary, isolated tow-path on horseback. For several months prior to the date of the holdup, he pointed out, it had gradually become customary for the other paymasters, as well as for himself, to go the dangerous route "unprotected and alone." No, sir, he wasn't surprised, not one little bit, that the bandits had jumped him. He firmly believed that they had been plotting the robbery for a long time, just as they had said – perhaps they had seen him at Tom Peden's saloon and stalked him and the saddlebag the whole distance down the tow-path from Campbell and Coat bank. On and on he went, telling of his six long years as a faithful paymaster, recounting details, describing the horses, the bandits, and his fright as he looked down the barrels of those three six-guns. No doubt about it, he added, he owed his life to the one kindly robber who had refused to let "his buddies" kill him, and the same one who had made the others return his watch and part of his personal money. . .

Everyone in the tense courtroom agreed that Alexander G. Smith and his moment had met. But when Judge Harry Bruce asked him definitely and without the shadow of a doubt to identify Frank James as one of the men who had robbed him on March 11, 1881 at about four o'clock in the afternoon, the paymaster could only reply, minus theatrics, that he "thought" he was, but in all truth he was "not positive."

I quote now from **The Huntsville Historical Review Vol 2, April 1972 Number 2 pages 9-10**, by Leland R. Johnson.

General Leroy Pope Walker, formerly Confederate Secretary of War, was chief counsel for James. He was assisted by Raymond B. Sloan of Nashville, Tennessee, and Richard Walker of Huntsville. Their fees were probably paid by a Confederate veterans organization, though the federal government paid the expenses of witnesses for the defense because James claimed he was unable to do so. United States District Attorney **William H. Smith**, former Reconstruction governor of Alabama, was chief prosecutor; he was assisted by **Captain Lionel W. Day**, former Assistant District Attorney. Judge **Harry Bruce** presided impartially over what promised to be a melodramatic confrontation, for both Governor William H. Smith and General Leroy P. Walker were capable of fiery courtroom oratory.

The trial was to begin on April 16, and the courtroom was crowded to capacity, but some of the witnesses from Nashville did not appear and the trial was postponed until the following day. On April 17 the court was again packed with spectators when the selection of the jury began. General Walker and Governor Smith immediately plunged into quarrels over legal technicalities, much to the satisfaction of the crowd, but the selection went quickly and all twelve jurymen were seated in the morning. A reporter described them as "a very fair looking body, most of them evidently from the country."

After the jury had been seated, the legal skirmishing began in earnest. General Walker, whose long gray beard gave him an air of "utmost distinction" was constantly picking apart the prosecution. A reporter described him as the "most notable figure" in the courtroom. Governor Smith, chief prosecutor called his first witness, **Thomas Peden**, who was to identify Frank James as one of the robbers.

Peden owned a saloon near Muscle Shoals Canal which was frequented by many of the visitors who came to see the project under construction.

Mr. Peden's testimony has been relayed in other sections.

The prosecution next called **Alexander G. Smith**, the government paymaster. His testimony was also relayed earlier.

The last witness of the first day, **J. N. Wilcoxon**, testified that he had met three strangers on the day of the robbery, but his description of them differed materially from that of the first two witnesses. By the end of the day, the attorneys for the defense were confident of acquittal.

Dick Liddil was called to the stand the following morning . Liddil, previously was convicted for complicity in the crime as a member of the James Gang, had agreed with Missouri authorities to testify against James in the Muscle Shoals case. General Walker objected to the admission of Liddil's testimony because Liddil had been convicted of stealing a horse in Missouri. The prosecution replied that Liddil had been pardoned for that offense and produced the papers to prove it. Judge Bruce allowed the testimony.

Liddil swore that William Ryan and Frank and Jesse had left Nashville on March 6, 1881. He stated that the two brothers were wearing sandy beards and Ryan a black beard when they left Nashville, and when they returned several days later they were wearing only moustaches and sideburns. He swore that they remained in Nashville until they learned of the capture of Ryan, and then rode north to stay with friends in Logan County, Kentucky. These friends, Silas Norris and Sarah Hite, were brought to the stand to confirm the later part of Liddil's testimony.

By Saturday, public sentiment in Huntsville was running strongly in favor of Frank James. The trial was the only subject of discussion among the customary Saturday visitors to town. A reporter observed that the people "gather in knots on the corners and argue legal points as if they held a consulting connection with the counsel in the case." No one believed Dick Liddil. He had a shifty look about him, and freely admitted that he was being paid by Missouri officials to testify against James. Many spectators, said a reporter," openly declare that they would not believe him on oath whatever the circumstances."

The prosecution presented its last two witnesses on Saturday. Hugh Riley, the bartender at Peden's saloon, confirmed the story of Tom Peden; Alfred Hill testified that three men stayed at his house north of the canal before the robbery and made inquiry about the date the employees were paid. Neither, however, could do more than say that Frank James resembled one of the men.

Article by Max York in **The Nashville Tennessean Magazine**, February 28, 1971.

We now pick up from Max York of the Nashville Tennessean Magazine.

The Nashville American had a reporter on hand (**For The Frank James Trial**). Since this was before bylines became popular, we do not know his name. However, he obviously was enjoying himself. This was a big story.

That afternoon, he wired a story to his morning paper. Several people, he said, had arrived from Nashville to testify for Frank James. **John Taylor, H. J. Fields, William H. Spann, Robert Dale (*Dole*)** and others had come from Nashville at government expense, since James had sworn that he was too poor to pay their expenses.

The witnesses, he said, would show that James had lived in Nashville as a hard working, steady citizen from 1877 until March 16, 1881. They would testify that James was in Nashville at the time of the robbery.

The defense called as its first witness **Sam Fields** a Nashville detective. Fields said that he had known Frank – as Ben Woodson – since 1879. Frank was hauling hogs for the Indiana Lumber Company (located on the river in East Nashville) in Nashville.

He said that He – Frank – was in Nashville that day. He said he knew it was that day because of a particular case – Stephens vs. Chickering – was being heard that day in the office of Bailey Brown, a justice of the peace.

"James, myself, **Dave Pittman and Theodore Willard** walked up Cherry Street, (4th Avenue) after the hearing," Fields said. "I also met him at Jonas Taylor's Shop (located on what is now Third Avenue) and saw him in front of Fisher's saloon." (Charlotte Avenue)

He said he had met J. D. Howard, and learned later he was Jesse James.

Jonas Taylor would testify that he met Ben Woodson in Nashville in 1878. They were introduced by Berry Cheatham. He said Woodson lived on the Drake place on White's Creek and later on the Smith place and again nearer town.

"J. D. Howard owned two horses in partnership with me," he said, They were named Jim Scott and Col. Hull. We bought them on credit from Jim Malone and Morris Landers. We raced the horses at fairs. Frank was in the shop on the 11th and 12th. I saw him five or 10 days later. He dropped by to say goodbye. He said he was going to Florida. Jesse kept a boarding house near the race track."

Taylor held up the books from his shop to prove Woodson had been in his shop on those days. The next Monday, the day began with R. B. Sloan, one of James attorneys, testifying that the books were in the same condition as when he first saw them when he was investigating James on a case in Gallatin, Missouri. He knew Woodson slightly in Nashville. He recalled Howard had a celebrated race horse named Jim Malone. He never saw Woodson and Howard together, he said. As for the boarding house, when he knew about it, it was operated by a Mrs. Snowden, and it was a house of bad repute. The court had taken it over and rented it to laborers.

J. Bailey Brown, the justice of the peace, brought his books to show that Stephens vs. Chickering was being tried before him on the 11th and 12th.

The Huntsville Historical Review Vol 2, April 1972 Number 2 page 11, by Leland R. Johnson.

One brief comment form the Huntsville Historical review and then back to the Nashville Tennessean Magazine.

The prosecution examined them (*Taylor's books*) and pointed out the different handwritings in which entries were made, the mutilated and smeared condition of the book, and the fact that the entries for March 11 and 12 were not made in the same column as previous entries. Taylor explained that he could now write so his books were kept for him by friends and these particular accounts had been in a fire since 1881.

Now back to Max York of the Nashville Tennessean Magazine –

W. H. Spann testimony was that he knew Woodson when he lived on Hyde's Ferry Pike and afterwards in Edgefield (East Nashville).

"In 1880, he lived on the Jeff Hyde place a quarter of a mile from me," Spann said. "I saw him often in '80 and early '81. He farmed and later hauled hogs. I was driving his mules and wagon with my brother in laws horse tied behind in February when I was in a ferry accident. The horse and the rear of the wagon was lost. I saw him in Nashville on the 12th to talk about the pedigree of some hogs I had bought from John Harvey."

Spann's brother in law, **Robert Dole**, ran a grocery store next to Jeff Hyde's place. He corroborated the accident story.

Jack Smith, a Negro (railroad) detective for **Maj. Geddes**, said he saw James on Deadrick Street the day of the robbery and on the corner of College (Third) and Union the next day.

On Tuesday, Walker, James' attorney, was ill, but our reporter took the opportunity to declare the opinion of Huntsville favored acquittal. Word was that once acquitted, James was going back to Missouri to visit his mother. On the way, he was going to stop off in Nashville to visit with his friends.

On Wednesday, the prosecution called **J. W. Davis**, who lived 10 miles west of Florence. He was in Peden's saloon that day. He described the strange men and horses that he saw.

Mrs. E. A. Jones of Columbia, Tennessee, was called. In 1881, she lived in Laurel Hill, Tennessee. Two or three days before the robbery, three men spent the night at her house. They left after breakfast. They wanted to know the way to Muscle Shoals.

The weather was too wet for farmers to tend their fields, so on the final days of the trial, they came to town to get a glimpse of Frank James.

The reporter talked with one of Mrs. James' friends.

"Mrs. James is so confident and cheerful," the friend said." "Should the verdict be anything but acquittal, it will kill her."

Mrs. James, a petite brunette, was the only woman spectator during the whole trial.

The American reporter found time to talk with James about a rumor he was going to get Dick Liddil when he was freed.

"Dick Liddil has nothing to fear from me," James said. "I try not to think of him. When I recall what he has done to me, it makes me feel fearful. Why, I wouldn't dirty my hands with him. If he had any manhood whatever, he would hang himself, like Judas."

James had received a postcard with a drawing of a gallows and a skull and crossbones. It said "if the jury at Huntsville don't hang you, you will not escape us." It was signed: Ford Brothers. It was postmarked Nashville. The reporter figured it was a prank.

"My hands don't much look like they could handle a plow and hoe, but they will get used to it again" James said.

James had recited scenes from Shakespeare for those who came to see him. People brought him apples and bouquets every day. He wore a gold ring that was the gift of one admirer. The black suit he was wearing was a gift from a Missouri newsman. The only money he had was some his wartime comrades sent him from Missouri.

W. Stanley Hoole, THE JAMES BOYS RODE SOUTH, FRANK AND JESSE JAMES AND THEIR COMRADES IN CRIME, pages 42-45, 1955. Privately printed for the author in Tuscaloosa, Alabama.

We return to W. Stanley Hoole for the closing arguments and the verdict.

At three o'clock, before a courtroom packed and overflowing into crowded corridors, the distinguished former Secretary of War for the Confederate States of America rose to defend his humble client, former private Alexander Franklin James of the Confederate States Army. Measuring his words slowly, the general plied argument upon argument, his deductions surpassing those of "any advocate" ever heard in Huntsville. His facts, tersely stated, were undeniable. Twice he turned to the defendant's wife and little child, in tearful tones bespeaking their gentility and poise an appealing for the freedom of their beloved husband and tender father, a gentleman wrongly accused and oft humiliated.

Then, after a grand pause, came the old soldier's grand strategy. He knew the jurymen to be Confederate veterans, most of them his personal friends. He knew they remembered him best, not as a lawyer, but as their former comrade-in-arms for the South. He knew their love for the Lost Cause and all who had fought for it. Skillfully, he began to capitalize on these facts.

Leaning informally over the jury bar, he reminded the twelve that he was proud of the privilege of serving the defendant, not only because he believed him innocent of all charges, but also because he was a Confederate – a man who had bravely come to the aid of the South in its great hour of need. He told of how Alexander Franklin James, as a lad in his teens, had enlisted in the Missouri State Guards, a Confederate regiment under the command of General Sterling Price. He describes Frank's fierce fight against the Yankees at the Battle of Wilson's Creek, near Springfield, Missouri on August 10, 1861 – The first important clash of arms, save First Bull Run, in the War for Southern Independence. He told of Frank's subsequent capture by the Federals, his jail sentence and ultimate escape to join Quantrill's Black Flag Brigade (the bloodiest band in the annals of the Confederacy), his participation in the famous Lawrence, Kansas raid, his everlasting battle against Yankee Jayhawkers all across the length and breadth of the Missouri-Kansas border country, and love for the Southland. (Actually, Frank did not surrender to the United States Army until June 26, at Samuel's Depot, Nelson County, Kentucky, more than three months *after* General Lee met General Grant at Appomattox. April 9, 1865.)

In low, whispered tones General Walker then electrified the hushed courtroom with cruel details of how Yankee militia had retaliated against Confederate Frank James by horse-whipping his fifteen-year-old brother Jesse and hanging his aged stepfather to a tree, while they tossed hand grenades into his home, setting it a-fire, blowing off his mother's right arm at the elbow and instantly killing his little half brother, Archie – all because they were Southern sympathizers. (It should be added the general somewhat overextended himself here, for the bomb in question was not thrown until January, 1875 and then by railroad detectives, not by soldiers. The jurymen evidently believed the worse however – or was it the best?)

Everyone agreed that General Walker's defense was the "ablest of many able speeches" the great Confederate warrior and barrister had ever delivered and through it all, the *Democrat* added "Mr. And Mrs. James sat cool, calm and collected . . . Slight flushes playing now and then on their pale but unmoved faces."

Shortly before six o'clock in the afternoon – it was Friday April 18, 1884, Judge Harry Bruce gave the jury a "very clear, fair and impartial charge" and the twelve old Confederates, good men and true, filed out one after the other, slowly and solemnly. Almost immediately, they returned, their decision reached: *Not Guilty*. And as Judge Bruce rapped his gavel, shouting "The defendant is discharged!"

Instantly, the crowd "loudly applauded" and shouts rang through the courtroom and down the hallways, for the verdict was "almost universally approved." (The *Democrat* reporter added, however, that *he* thought such ungenteel enthusiasm "exceedingly wrong.") A free man, Frank James rushed over and gratefully shook General Walker's hand. Admirers patted him on the back and Huntsville ladies gathered sympathetically about poor, weary Mrs. James and wide-eyed, innocent little Robert.

In the author's opinion, this was effectively the end of the James Gang. Jesse was dead, Frank was sidelined and the balance of the bandit group were either imprisoned or scattered so widely that they could never function as an outlaw society again.

Chapter 25

Frank James' Legal Problems Did Not End With The Huntsville Trial

W. Stanley Hoole, THE JAMES BOYS RODE SOUTH, FRANK AND JESSE JAMES AND THEIR COMRADES IN CRIME, page 46-47, 1955. Privately printed for the author in Tuscaloosa, Alabama.

W. Stanley Hoole relays that unfortunately, as the former bandit walked out into the Alabama sunlight, he was instantly re-arrested by **Sheriff Frank Rogers** of Boonville, Cooper County, Missouri. The sheriff had been lurking about Huntsville for several days under an assumed name. (Another sheriff from Northfield, Minnesota was there to grab Frank also, but he was a little too late, according to the newspapers.) The next day at two o'clock, a prisoner once more, Frank was hustled aboard the train for Missouri, under armed guard.

By now, however, the public sentiment had grown strong in favor of forever freeing Frank James. Why another trial? Why drag the unfortunate man through court after court, year after year? Hadn't he been punished enough? After all, the crimes of which he had been accused were but aftermaths of war, a bitter conflict that flamed men's passions and shaped their reasons. Everyone agreed that the times were different now…

And so they were. Seven Missourians signed Frank's bond and the Boonville indictment yellowed on the record books. In 1885 it was officially "forgotten" and the famous bandit became a full-fledged citizen and a free man. As such he lived for thirty years, a shoe salesman, a race track starter, a circus entertainer, a farmer – but always normally, unassumingly, and quietly. Bitterly ashamed of his days of outlawry, to the very end he was a man who believed in keeping his own counsel and respecting the privacy of others–like any true Confederate gentleman.

Author's note: Frank James died of natural causes in 1915 – or did he?

In the **July 25, 1993 issue of the Montgomery Advertiser** Mr. Nick Lackeos has a little different opinion about this. I quote from this article:

After Frank was acquitted at a Huntsville trial for a Muscle Shoals robbery, he was released by authorities and died some 30 years later of natural causes in 1915.

Or did he?

During the first half of this century, questions would occasionally arise about whether Jesse and Frank were really dead. **Mr. Bradley**, head of special collections at the Alabama Department of Archives and History, believes they were.

On the other hand, **Wayne Greenhaw**, director of the Alabama Department of Tourism and Travel isn't so sure – not about Frank anyway.

"When I was a boy, I remember an old man that came to our school and talked to us," said Mr. Greenhaw. That year was 1948 (*Frank James would have been 105 years old at that time*) in North Alabama. "And he said he was Frank James. I was in elementary school. It was in Trussville, just east of Birmingham."

"The teacher felt that even though the old man was a reformed criminal it would be an opportunity for the children to meet someone who had once been an outlaw in the Wild West and to hear him talk about his place in history, even though he was an infamous robber of banks and trains," said Mr. Greenhaw.

"He had white hair and a white moustache, kind of scraggly looking," said Mr. Greenhaw.

"He was a kindly looking old fellow – about medium build. He was wearing a dark suit and a string tie like the Western folks wear.

He talked to us about how he and his brother, Jesse, would come to Alabama and hide out and rest. They were friends with a North Alabama outlaw – **Rube Burrow**.

Rube Burrow also robbed trains and he had hideouts in places where they stayed up in the hills of North Alabama. There's a hill that runs south of Muscle Shoals and there's a canyon on top of that hill. Its south of Russellville and near a community called Phil Campbell.

It's beautiful country up there. There's a creek or little river that runs through the canyon. So they had fresh water. It has white water in places where people go canoeing.

And even this time of year when it gets hot, it gets cool down there in the canyon. It has magnificent foliage and ferns. You still have virgin pine trees and oaks up there. And that was their hideout in that canyon on top of that hill.

According to that old man, he and his brother hung out with Rube Burrow up there and stayed away from the law.

Mr. Greenhaw also heard outlaw stories about that area from another source.

"I had an old buddy – he was my age and he was up there in Russellville. He died a couple of years ago, but he was quite a storyteller. And he would tell stories of what his relatives had told him about the James brothers riding into Alabama to stay with kinfolks.

He would tell us stories about Frank and Jesse riding in with their long coats. I didn't pay much attention to him then."

Author's note: It seems conspiracy stories abounded back then and are still with us even today!

From a page on the internet hosted by **Mr. Donald Greyfield**. He has several photographs of where Frank James and Annie are buried. It is well worth visiting as it offers much more to the reader than is quoted here:

Alexander Franklin James
Born January 10, 1843
Died February 18, 1915

"With creeping old age, Frank James returned to the James' farm giving tours for the price of twenty-five cents. Here Frank James died on February 18, 1915 at the age of 72.

Frank was cremated because he feared grave robbers. His ashes were kept in a bank vault until his wife's death at age 91 in 1944. She was cremated and the couple was interred in Hill Park Cemetery, which is located in the upper part of Hill Park, Independence, Missouri and consists of a small stone wall enclosure of graves."

In the author's opinion, this was the very end of the James Gang. The last of the James Gang, Frank James, had departed to meet his maker for his final judgment.

Chapter 26

Play

"Muscle Shoals Alabama Payroll Robbery"

The Beginning of the End for the James Gang

A play written by the Jackson County Advanced Creative Writers' Group made up of Ilena Holder, Cathy Palmer and R. G. "Jerry" Tidwell for the town of Killen, Alabama. This play was written for the Town of Killen to present at their amphitheater.

The Beginning of the End For The James Gang

Act 1- The Planning Meeting at the Saloon.

Characters: Frank James, Jesse James, "Wild Bill" Ryan, Hugh Riley, bar keeper, Thomas Peden.

[Casting and wardrobe note]: From published sources:

Frank James: Photographs of Frank James show he was completely bald on top. He supposedly went bald at age 55. He had to be seriously balding if not bald when the Muscle Shoals payroll robbery took place in April 1881.

He was generally dressed in dark clothes, long coat, and (when on a raid) wearing a black slouch hat.

Frank James was reputedly about six feet tall and slender. He walked erect, with a quiet, easy and self-possessed gait. He always had a look of self-repose. Frank laughed - not at all. He was sober, sedate, a splendid man always for ambush or scouting parties – from Noted Guerrillas, Edwards, John Newman, an old book, copyrighted in 1877, obtainable in various forms on the internet.

Jesse James was five feet 11 (10 from another source) and one half inches tall. He weighed 195 pounds and stood very straight.

When on a raid, he dressed very common in a dark calico shirt and ducking overalls, pants leg in boots. - Testimony of Dick Liddil

Jesse laughed at many things – was light-hearted, reckless, with a devil may-care attitude.   - Noted Guerrillas

[Photographs and other information for the other characters in this play will be provided with the manuscript.]

Setting: Morning, the Thomas Peden Saloon at Lock Three near Killen, Alabama.

Curtain opens.

Opening scene: Thomas Peden on stage, sitting in rocking chair, coffee cup in hand, talking to Hugh Riley, also with coffee cup. Saloon is empty behind them.

Peden: The lock is coming along fine. It's given a lot of men folks jobs around here.

H. Riley: Yup, it's hard work, but steady. And they pay you in cash! Couldn't ask any better than that!

Peden: Times are hard around here, even with the war over. A man's still gotta feed his family.

H. Riley: Tell me about it. I've got 5 young 'uns to feed and my wife's laid up in bed right now with some female problem. Her maw's tending to her. If she doesn't get better soon, we're goin' to call the doctor in. She traveled here from Huntsville to take care of her. I sure couldn't. That's why I'm here at the saloon now. To get away from all them women folks!

Peden: I saw you got here extra early today. Who's taking care of the kids while you're here?

H. Riley: The oldest girl. She's got enough sense to watch'em.

Peden: I've got to say that business has been good. You know that Hugh. We get a steady stream of curious folks most every day. I bet there's thirty or so every week. Everybody wants to know about the locks and the progress.

H. Riley: And they <u>all</u> stop here to talk and get drinks. I'm glad you gave me a job, Tom.

Peden: How come you haven't gone out to the lock and seen if they're hiring? I hear it pays real good. I know that paymaster Smith says so. He's a good Scotchman.

H. Riley: I'm too old to do work like that, plus I have a bad back. Tending bar is easy on me. I might work at the lock if I was a younger man. Just the very thought of working a shovel and pick ax all day plumb wears me out.

[both men laugh]

[James brothers and Wild Bill ride their horses up and tie them under a shade tree. They look around. Frank and Wild Bill enter the saloon through side door].

Peden: You'd better go inside Hugh. We've got some paying customers.

H. Riley: Yes, sir. [He gets up and goes inside the bar. Jesse James sits down in the empty chair and talks to Peden.]

Peden: How are you doing today, sir?

J. James: Right fine. We'd like some drinks and a little food.

Peden: My man Hugh will serve everyone when he gets their orders. I've been seeing you men around here the last couple of weeks, haven't I? [he eyes Jesse up and down.]

J. James: My friend and I are revenue agents. The other man is a fruit tree peddler.

Peden: Oh, I see. Revenue agents.

J. James: What do you think of our new President?

Peden: You mean James A. Garfield? Too soon to tell I reckon.

J. James: I think he'll do fine. You know, I've been to Washington recently and met up with Robert Todd Lincoln.

Peden: You mean Abe's son?

J. James: Yes, the new head of the War Department.

Peden: Don't say? [he's obviously impressed that James knows Abe Lincoln's son.]

J. James: Just the other day I received a letter from William Windom. He said he wanted me to visit him as soon as possible.

Peden: Windom you say? The head of the Treasury Department? [still in awe]

J. James: [hitching his chair closer to PEDEN] Now, man to man I want to ask you about the slaves. How have things been going around here? Are they still easy to manage since the war ended?

Peden: I guess you could say so. I haven't seen many differences.

J. James: Good. So you'd say the cotton crop won't be affected?

Peden: I don't think so. Some of the slaves stayed on to farm for themselves.

J. James: I'm powerful thirsty. I think I'll go inside now. What kind of whiskey do you keep here? [Both men go inside. Attention focuses on others now.]

H. Riley: What'll you boys be having? You sure are out and about early today.

Jesse: We just got in from Atlas.

H. Riley: Atlas? Got family there?

Jesse: We were visiting Alfred Hill for three nights.

H. Riley: Oh, I don't know him personally.

Frank: [interrupting abruptly as if to shut Jesse up] We're hungry. What do ya'll have to eat?

H. Riley: We've got a few things put back. [He goes to a big barrel and gets crackers out, putting them on a plate.] We've been having so many people stop here and look at the locks we're finding we need to keep more food on hand than before. What did you boys say your names were?

Jesse [grunting]: We didn't.

Wild Bill: You got any cheese to go with that?

Bartender: Sure do. [He reaches behind the bar and takes a slab of cheese wrapped up in paper, then cuts off some pieces of equal sizes.] Fresh cheddar-- just had it delivered two days ago.

[At this point, the gang is seated and has removed their hats. They begin to relax.]

Jesse: What's to drink?

Bartender: All I've got today is whiskey or applejack. We're fresh out of beer, but I've got a delivery due tomorrow.

Wild Bill: I'll take a shot of the applejack.

Frank: I'll take the whiskey.

[The gang moves to the far side of the tavern so they can talk privately.]

Jesse: How do you think this'll go down? You know the paymaster will be heavily armed.

Frank: Yup. Robbin' sure ain't what it used to be. You know how the Youngers got killed up in Minnesota.

[H. Riley - brings drinks and food to the table. Retreats silently back to the bar area.]

Wild Bill: Well here's a map I sketched out. [He spreads a small map out so the men can see.] It'll get us back to the state line after the robbery.

Frank: [Looks over his shoulder to see if Peden and Hugh are within earshot, then looks at the map.] This is the road he'll be riding up here on. Every week on the same day he brings the payroll from Florence. Today's the day boys. [He draws his finger down the map.] And this is where I think we should ambush him. [He points to another spot on the map marked with an "X"]

Jesse: Why did you pick that spot?

Frank: Because he'll have to stop, dismount and then open a gate. And when he starts to mount, we'll ride out of the bushes and surprise him.

Wild Bill: Y'all know he'll be armed.

Jesse: I've seen his holster on his hip since I've been watching him come and go. He never travels without his gun.

Frank: He never gets an escort either. Smith always travels alone with his pay pouch. Most all of the ones we've robbed in the past have been armed. Didn't stop us none, did it? It is appointed unto men once to die.

Wild Bill: How much longer do you think we'll keep on living this way?

Frank: Jesse and I've been doing it twenty years now. Haven't got stopped yet. [All the men laugh except Frank James.]

Wild Bill: I'm just saying one day our luck might run out. We haven't done any robbin' in four years. We're getting rusty.

Frank: That's why we plan it out beforehand, Bill. Escape routes, plenty of firearms, and young, fresh fleet-footed horses.

Jesse: This is the day it goes down. We've been hanging around this lock for three weeks now. We can't stall anymore or people'll be getting suspicious of us.

Frank: We'll wait until later in the afternoon. Loaf around some you know. Then after we hit our mark, we'll hide out in the woods. I've got the compass so we'll know what direction we're headed in. That'll give us some cover in the dark until we can put some distance between us and this place.

Wild Bill: Let's go boys. We've got the rest of the day to check out those back roads again.

[The men stand. Wild Bill tucks his map into his shirt pocket. Frank tucks his compass into his pants pocket. Wild Bill and Frank go outside. Jesse walks to the bar.]

149

JESSE: [to Hugh Riley] What do we owe you for the food and drinks?

Hugh Riley: Uh, for the three of you just a dollar. [Jesse takes a coin out of his pocket and lays it on the bar.]

JESSE: Thank you much. [He turns and follows the other two men.]
Hugh Riley: [goes to front door and watches the men ride off. He returns inside and cleans off the table.]

Thomas Peden: [comes back to stage, carrying a whiskey crate] Those fellers ride off? [to H. Riley]

Hugh Riley: [carrying tray back to bar with glasses, bottles, plates] Yep. They left their money on the bar.

Thomas Peden: Kind of quiet gentlemen if you ask me. Well, they said they were revenue agents so maybe they have to keep their mouths shut. I wonder what else will happen today.

Hugh Riley: [wiping hands on a towel] Can't rightly say. It's payday at the Lock, so we'll probably have lot of men drinkin' in here tonight.

Thomas Peden: You're right, Hugh, you're right. Every Friday there's a lot of money floating around this little place.

Curtain closes.

Act 2

Robbery

Characters: Frank James, Jesse James, Wild Bill Ryan, Alexander Smith

Narration:

Their reconnaissance done and all of the information gathered that they could get, the three men were now ready to commit the robbery. They rode to their selected location for the robbery to take place and awaited Alexander Smith's arrival with the payroll.

About this time Alexander G. Smith, United States Army Paymaster, strolled nonchalantly out of the William T. Campbell Banking Company in Florence, Alabama and hung a heavy saddlebag over his horse's back. Glancing quickly at his gold watch, he swung easily into his saddle and slowly galloped south down muddy Court street and turned east on the Muscle Shoals tow path toward the Engineer's Camp at Bluewater on the Tennessee River a few miles upstream from Florence and toward Rogersville. It was four o'clock on Friday afternoon, March 11, 1881.

A few minutes later, the horse was jogging unhurriedly along the tow path that paralleled the Muscle Shoals Canal, a scant two miles from Florence.

Scene 1: Robbery

Curtain opens.

Setting: Wooded and brushy area along the tow path that paralleled the Muscle Shoals Canal about 2 miles east of Florence.

[All three bandits are on foot at this point.]

Frank James: Bill, you go around and hide in the brush on the other side of the gate. It will cover you until Smith is right on top of you at that gate [motioning toward the gate]. It will be too late for him to reach for his pistol because you will spring from the brush at that place and be covering him with both of your pistols drawn and

151

cocked as soon as he opens the gate. Jesse and I will hide in the brush until you spring out. Then we will spring out from the brush behind him with our pistols drawn and cocked as well. We will have him completely surrounded and he will have to do as we tell him. We will shoot him at once if he does not obey us.

["Wild Bill" draws and cocks his pistols and hides in the brush beyond the gate. Frank and Jesse draw and cock their pistols and hide in the brush on the side of the gate that Smith will be approaching from. Hoof beats can be heard approaching and then stop abruptly. Smith enters the stage on foot and approaches the gate past Frank and Jesse.]

"Wild Bill": [springing from the brush after Smith opens the gate.] Freeze! Don't make a move for your gun or I will kill you.

[Frank and Jesse spring out of the brush behind Alexander Smith with their pistols pointed toward his head. Frank has the saddlebag in one hand and his drawn pistol in the other. Jesse's pistol is also drawn. Jesse disarms Smith.]

Frank James: What do we have here? [holding the saddle bag aloft] What do you have for us this fine afternoon?

"Wild Bill" Ryan: [ties Smith's hands together behind his back and searches him] Look'ee what I have found! [As he holds up the $221 and a gold watch he found on Alexander Smith's person. This causes a quick whispered conference among the bandits.]

Frank James: How much of this money is yours and how much is the government's?

Alexander Smith: I had $21.00 of my own when I went to the bank and the rest of what you took out of my pocket is my pay.

Frank James [after a second whispered conference]: We only want the government's money not yours. [As he returns $21.00 to Smith's pocket along with the gold watch.]

Jesse James: We have to get going - we have a long way to ride. You ride in front behind me [motioning to Smith] and don't try any funny business as someone will be right behind you and will shoot you if they have to.

Jesse James [holding a business card toward Smith just before they all mount up again and reads it to Smith before also putting it in his pocket.]

Jesse James: I am yours truly Henry Smith! Just who in the devil are you? ["Wild Bill" joins heartily in the laughter.]

["Wild Bill" and Jesse exit the stage still laughing. Frank James and Smith exit last and are not laughing.]

Curtain closes.

Narration:

Silently the four horsemen wind their way through the wild, deserted forest, a wilderness unbroken save the work camps of the Unites States Engineers at intervals of several miles along the Muscle Shoals Canal. At dusk, the robbers remove their masks and become talkative.

Scene 2: Ride Toward Tennessee

Similar setting as first scene without the gate: The gang is taking a break from riding. Jesse James, "Wild Bill" and Alexander Smith with hands still tied enter the stage. The bandits have all removed their masks.

Curtain opens.

Wild Bill: I'm glad we took a break. I needed to stretch my legs.

Jesse James: [turning to Smith] We're all Texans. We've been lurking in the neighborhood, plotting this payroll robbery for more than a week.

"Wild Bill": We have passed through the canal zone more than once on missions into South Alabama.

Alexander Smith: You certainly seem to understand the country pretty well!

Frank James: [entering the stage] Well, we should. We have spent a lot of time around here.

Alexander Smith: How about untying me? You have my gun and there are three of you. I can't do anything. You surely don't think that I can overpower you.

Jesse James: Not for now. Maybe later.

Alexander Smith: What do you plan to do with me? I am no danger to you. You have the money and that is all that you wanted. You can get nothing else from me!

Jesse James: We'll figger all of that out later.

Frank James: Time to get moving again [motions them off the stage.]

[They all exit.]

[The sound of loud hoof beats can be heard offstage but they soon fade out.]

Curtain closes.

Narration:

As they rode on hour after hour, past Bull's Mill and Center Star and into the darkness of the forest, the bandits probed Paymaster Smith with questions and nervously bantered him with small talk. This time they told him they were Tennessee farmers – good ones, too. Smith later recalled that they were "dressed for the part."

In constant dread, Paymaster Smith could but frightfully marvel about the good-natured nonchalance of the desperados. One of the men, the oldest, seemed almost like a preacher, at times quoting bits from Shakespeare or the Bible. The second was a loud-mouthed braggart and the third, the youngest man, was talkative to be true, but sharp-eyed and ever alert.

Four hours and twenty miles after the hold-up the men stop in a dense, deeply secluded spot.

Scene 3: Dividing the Money

Setting: A similarly deserted wooded and brushy area

Curtain opens.

[All four men are on stage. The bandits are squatted in a circle on the ground. "Henry Smith" is dividing the money evenly among his partners and himself. Alexander Smith is sitting on the ground some distance away with his hands still tied.]

Frank James: It is indeed true. The Good Lord does help those who help themselves.

Jesse James: This was a fair take but not as much as I thought it would be.

Bill Ryan: It will be enough to last me a good while. I won't have any money problems for a good while!

Jesse James: Not the way you like whiskey. It will probably last you only one good drunk! [Jesse and "Wild Bill" chuckle]

Bill Ryan: We should shoot the paymaster now to keep him quiet since he has brought us all this money. [He approaches Smith who is still sitting on the ground with two cocked pistols. He places the pistols to Smith's head.]

Frank James: We are not killers and I alone, if necessary, will permit no personal harm to the captive.

[This does not satisfy Bill Ryan who obeys and slowly backs away from Smith with pistols still drawn. He is still glaring menacingly at Smith.]

Frank James: If you do shoot him you had best have a bullet left for me for I will truly kill you!

["Wild Bill" holsters his guns, Frank and Jesse then untie Smith's hands. Frank James tosses Smith an overcoat as it is beginning to thunder.]

"Wild Bill": I still say we should kill him. He can tell everyone what we look like and which way we went.

Frank James: That is not your decision to make Bill. You are just a gun hand along for the ride.

Frank James: Pass the night comfortably Mr. Smith.

[Everyone except Alexander Smith exits the stage. Jesse James says before he exits] Let's mount up and get as far away from here as we can tonight. [Hoof beats can be heard as they ride off, soon tapering off into silence.]

[Alexander Smith stands alone looking around.]

Alexander Smith: I wonder just where in the blazes I am. Which is the way back to the Bluewater Camp? I wonder just how I will ever find my way back!

They've taken my horse and my gun. I'm alone and don't know where I am. All of these woods look the same in every direction.

[Alexander Smith wanders off stage still looking in all directions as he exits. Thunder can be heard again.]

Curtain closes.

Act 3 - Aftermath or the Muscle Shoals Robbery

Characters: "Wild Bill" Ryan, James McGinnis (customer at bar), W. L. Earthman (barkeeper and owner), Alexander Smith, unnamed Nashville Police Detective, unnamed Nashville policeman

Narration:

The three bandits return to the Nashville, Tennessee area after the Muscle Shoals robbery. Frank and Jesse James return home while "Wild Bill" Ryan goes to hide out at the Hite farm in Adairsville, near Russellville, Logan County, Kentucky.

The Muscle Shoals robbery was a perfect one - but its aftermath was a disaster for the James Gang.

On March 25, 1881, a well dressed stranger rides into White's Creek, a village near Nashville, Tennessee.

Opening Scene: Earthman's Grocery Store and Saloon

Curtain opens.

Setting: W. L. Earthman's bar in White's Creek Tennessee. W. L. Earthman is behind the bar while James McGinnis, a customer is standing in front of it. Several more unnamed patrons are sitting at a table in the background.

["Wild Bill" enters saloon by front door.]

Earthman: Come on in stranger. You have picked a nasty night to be out.

Wild Bill: Yeah, this thunderstorm just came up from nowhere.

Earthman: What'll you have?

"Wild Bill": [looking around before replying] A drink of whiskey and something to eat. What do you have?

157

Earthman: We have some raw oysters tonight and some good whiskey.

"Wild Bill": Sounds good to me! Bring it on!

[While Earthman is getting everything together James McGinnis turns to Wild Bill.]

McGinnis: What is your name stranger?

"Wild Bill": Hill, Tom Hill.

McGinnis: You from around here or passing through.

"Wild Bill": Passing through on my way back to Nashville from visiting friends in Kentucky.

[Earthman brings the drink and oysters and Wild Bill drinks the whiskey in one gulp.]

"Wild Bill": That was good. I'll have another. Keep 'em coming when the glass is empty!

[After six or seven drinks in quick succession "Wild Bill" is getting friendlier and more talkative.]

["Wild Bill" turns to McGinnis and starts up a conversation.]

"Wild Bill": What do you do friend?

McGinnis: I'm a farmer and raise cattle.

"Wild Bill": You don't say? How many head do you have?

McGinnis: About two dozen. Several of the heifers are about to drop calves.

"Wild Bill" [Slurring his words]: "I'll bet you are happy about that.

McGinnis: Sure am! What do you do Tom?

["Wild Bill" thinks for a minute before replying, slurring his words even more now.]

"Wild Bill": I'll tell you what friend… [Wild Bill replies in a loud voice. He turns to Earthman and replies in even a louder voice.]

"Wild Bill": I have been an outlaw against State, county and the Federal Government. I am now working as a detective for the U.S. government.

Earthman: Now, now, calm down a little bit. You don't seem like that kind of a feller. You have had enough to drink and should be moving along. The rain has stopped. We run a peaceable place here.

[This enrages "Wild Bill" who then, in a drunken stupor, draws two pistols and fires two rounds into the ceiling.]

Earthman: We'll have none of that here. I am a Justice of the Peace of Davidson County and have been a Constable but will ignore it this time if you will just move along.

[McGinnis and some of the customers in the background start to move in on "Wild Bill" from behind. Earthman's reply has enraged Wild Bill even more. He fires two more shots into the ceiling at which time the customers move in and subdue him after a brief scuffle.]

["Wild Bill" is relieved of his two pistols and two patrons hold him while Earthman pats him down. Wild Bill is still struggling.]

Earthman: What do we have here? [Earthman exclaims while pulling a large sum of money from "Tom Hill's" pockets. Earthman starts to count the money while the patrons tie Wild Bill's hands and feet, while "Wild Bill" is struggling trying to get free but to no avail. He is grunting and yelling at anyone in earshot.]

"Wild Bill": LET ME GO! I will kill all of you as soon as I get free!

Earthman: He had about $1500 on him and two pistols. We'll have to hold him until we can turn him over to the Nashville Police. Some of you boys take him out to the barn and lock him up in the corn crib. Stand guard over him till the Nashville police pick him up!

[The patrons exit the stage dragging "Wild Bill" who is still struggling while Earthman starts to put the money and pistols away.]

Curtain closes.

Scene 2: Nashville Jail

Narration:

A heavily built man, unwashed and unshaven for days and smelling like a pot still, lay huddled on a verminous blanket in a corner of a cell in the Nashville jail – a mass of human misery.

Curtain opens.

Sctting: A Nashville jail cell.

[Wild Bill is alone on stage in a jail cell, huddled on the filthy blanket. He rises slowly and starts talking to himself while staggering about the floor.]

Wild Bill: That was one wheel-horse of a drunk that I have been on and it has left me with one whale of a hangover. [He shakes his head to try to clear the cobwebs.] How am I ever goin' to talk myself out of this mess the bottle done got me in this time? The drunk charge, and the other one of shootin' up the saloon don't bother me none, they don't mount to anything more than a scrape. But the money – or the best part of it anyway– that I got as my share of that job down in Muscle Shoals is missing. Hell, even I can't drink up $1500 worth whiskey in just over a week. The law must have taken it off me. And that means a lot of questions about a lot of things I'd just as well not discuss.

Well, in this business you just got to look out for number one because ain't nobody else goin' to do it for you. Besides Jesse and that stuck-up Frank ain't even been around to see about me. If old "Wild Bill" Ryan gits out of this mess, I'll just have to help myself!

But what am I goin' to have to do?

[Enter the Chief of Detectives.]

[The Chief of Detectives starts questioning the prisoner through the bars of the jail cell. Wild Bill is still drunk and disheveled from the night before. The filthy blanket is still heaped up in the corner.]

Detective: Man, you look a mess this morning! Just who are you anyway? Earthman said you claimed to be Tom Hill.

[Wild Bill refuses to speak. He just stares blankly ahead.]

Detective: How did you come to have all of this money on you?

[Wild Bill has no reply.]

Detective: You may as well as tell me. We will find out anyway.

[Wild Bill remains silent, but he averts his eyes to the side this time.]

Detective: We wired your description all around and it is just a matter of time before we hear who you are and what you have been up to. Were you part of the gang that pulled that Muscle Shoals Payroll robbery the other day? Some of us think you are. What do you have to say about that?

[Wild Bill is visibly shaken but will still not say anything. He is getting more sober but is still pretty drunk. He staggers around.]

Detective: We have the paymaster that was robbed coming in here today to see if he can identify you.

[Wild Bill remains silent.]

[Enter a Nashville Policeman with a telegram.]

Detective: What do you have here?

Policeman: We heard from that wire to Missouri. They say that Tom Hill is none other than William Ryan, alias Jack Ryan, known to some as "Whiskey Head" Ryan, a member of the notorious Jesse James Gang.

Detective: "Whiskey Head" Ryan 'eh? That name sure fit's the way he smells right now! [both policemen chuckle.]

[The two policemen exit the stage chuckling. Bill Ryan is left alone on stage in his cell for a few minutes.]

"Wild Bill": [talking to himself and shaking his head as if in disbelief] How am I goin' to get out of this mess? They know who I am and that I am a member of the James Gang. What can I tell them that they will believe and get me out of this mess? "Oh Lord!" [He says with his head raised skyward] "If I ever get out of this mess I swear I'll never touch another drop as long as I live! I swear." [he adds softly with his head downcast.]

[Enter stage the Detective and Alexander Smith.]

Detective: Is this one of the men who robbed you?

Smith: He sure is! He is the one who wanted to shoot me in the head! He put those two big pistol barrels right up to my head. Those barrels looked as big as stove pipes. He would have shot me too if it had not been for the leader of that band of cutthroats!

Detective: Thanks, Mr. Smith. We will take care of him from here and be sure he is punished. I will notify the United States Marshals that we have him.

Curtain closes.

Act 4 - Flight Back To Missouri

Characters: Frank James, Jesse James, Dick Liddil, Clarence Hite, Zee James, boy and girl 10 - 12 years old

Set note: There are 4 scenes in this act. The first three are all in the living rooms of three different houses. The furniture can be moved around a little between each scene and different slipcovers can be thrown over the furniture.

Narration:

The day after "Wild Bill's" arrest was Saturday. Dick Liddil was at Jesse James' house that afternoon. Since Jesse thought it best to stay inside so soon after a robbery, Liddil went into Nashville to collect some money from the sale of some of Jesse's furniture. Taken from Liddil's testimony at the 1884 trial of Frank James in Huntsville, Alabama, Liddil said, "I got an evening paper, and saw from the description of the arrested man that it was Ryan. I went over and told Jesse and Frank."

For the ever increasingly edgy Jesse, this capture must have conjured up the ghost Hobbs Kerry. Hobbs was a simple-minded raw recruit who was left holding the horses during the Otterville, Missouri train robbery in 1876. Hobbs was captured during this robbery and promptly named everyone who had taken part in the robbery for the authorities.

The danger stemmed not only from the imprisoned bandit, but from the man who had made the arrest. The two James brothers knew W. L. Earthman personally having met him at a racetrack in 1879. It would not take him long to connect Ryan with the man he knew as J. D. Howard.

While "Wild Bill" Ryan was sweating it out in the Nashville jail, trying to construct a believable alibi for having about $1500 in gold and greenbacks on his person, a tall thin man rode out of the gate of his farm a few miles north of Nashville, bound for the home of Mr. Howard.

The horseman, whom the neighbors knew as B. J. (Ben) Woodson, raised Poland China hogs which he sold on the Nashville market. He also grew corn and grain to feed them, and in this late March of 1881, with planting season near, he needed some good mules. J. B. (Tom) Howard, who like himself, had lived in this Tennessee region but four years, was supposed to have some young but workable stock for sale.

But when Woodson reached the Howard farm, the price of mules never entered the conversation between the two stockmen.

Scene 1: Jesse James Living Room

Setting: Living room of the Howard farmhouse.

Curtain opens.

[Dick Liddil and Jesse are reading the paper and discussing Bill Ryan's arrest.]

Dick Liddil: I picked up this paper in Nashville and thought you would like to see it.

Jesse James: I sure do. That drunken Irishman has put us in a pickle now!

Dick Liddil: He sure has. What are you fixin to do now?

Jesse James: I don't know. We'll figure something out.

[Frank James enters the stage at this point.]

Frank James: Jesse, that damned Irishman of yours has done it now. He's been drunk now over a week and busted into Earthman's place, shot it up and popped off his mouth. They've got him in the Nashville jail now, and if I know Bill Ryan, he'll tell 'em anything to save his sorry hide!

[Jesse blinks his eyes, a nervous habit he had had since childhood and pauses a moment before answering.]

Jesse James: Frank, Bill's alright, 'long as he's sober; he just got too much liquor in him. But I don't guess we can take a chance. You and Annie get the boy ready, we got to get out of here. Maybe we better go ahead and let them and Zee foller with the kids. I'll meet you on the road.

Frank James: Slow down here Jesse. Let's think this through a little more. I'll send Annie and little Robert on to Kansas City by the train.

Jesse James: I'll send Zee and the children on to Donnie Pence's house in Nelson County, Kentucky.

Frank James: You, Dick and I will go to the Hite farm in Adairsville for a little while to see what happens around here.

Curtain closes.

Narration:

Thus ended for Frank and Jesse James the happiest years they had known since embarking on a crime career that was to make them world-infamous, enduring legends that are part of America's folk-lore. Had they resisted the temptation to rob the government payroll at Muscle Shoals, Alabama, less than a month before, they might have lived out their years in an uneasy kind of security in Middle Tennessee, well thought of by their neighbors and, with their wives and children, as ordinary members of an ordinary Southern community.

The Muscle Shoals payroll robbery was indeed the beginning of the end for the James gang. Each step they took from that point on brought them ever closer to their final demise.

It was three days after the Howards had fled the area before anyone in the immediate area knew they were missing. Then, when two men did ride that way, they found only an empty house with chickens scratching in the yard. They caught and trussed the latter, to take them home. But the Howards had left something else behind them. As the men rode away they saw under an old apple tree a double mound, with a large stone marker between them. It was the grave of the twins, born during their stay in the Nashville area.

Scene 2: Living room of Hite house

Setting: The Hite farmhouse in Adairsville, Logan County Kentucky.

Curtain opens.

[Frank James and Jesse James with Dick Liddil are lounging around the living room of the farmhouse with Clarence Hite standing guard outside.]

Jesse James: Frank, what do you think is happenin' back in Tennessee just now?

Frank James: I don't know, Jesse, but we'll send Dick Liddil back in a few days to find out.

Dick Liddil: Sure, I'll go check out everything for you. I'm getting kind of tired of just settin' around this place. That good-looking Mrs. George Hite ain't around anyhow.

[Clarence Hite comes running into the house through the front door.]

Clarence Hite: There are three heavily armed men headin' this way slowly and just lookin' around! [he exclaims excitedly]

 [Startled, everyone in the room scrambles to their feet, grab their rifles and shotguns and take defensive positions. Slow hoof beats can be heard outside, steadily getting louder at first and more muted as they ride by.]

Frank James [guarding the side parlor window]: We will be more than a match for them.

Jesse James [from beside the front window, anxiously]: I don't know who they are but we will give them trouble if they are looking for it.

Dick Liddil [from the hallway boastfully]: Let them come on!

[The group watched the three men slowly ride by without firing a shot. Jesse changed his position to the other side of the front window after the men ride by the house. They continue to watch from their vantage points as the men disappear.]

Frank James: I don't know who those men were but they sure looked the house over real good.

Jesse James [nervously]: I think we had better clear out of here.

Frank James: I agree. They were looking everything over too well just to be out for a casual ride.

Frank James [turning to Clarence]: Clarence, go back outside and continue to stand watch.

[Clarence exits the stage the way he came in.]

Jesse James: We should join Zee and the kids at Donny Pence's place.

Frank James: We will wait till dark to be safe.

Curtain closes.

Narration:

What those inside could not know, the three men who rode past the Hite house were indeed looking for them. In the wake of the Muscle Shoals robbery and Ryan's capture, Deputy U. S. Marshal W. S. Overton tracked the James brothers back to Tennessee and followed them on their flight to the Hite house in Adairsville. With two hired guns, James B. Murphy and A. J. Sullivan, it was these three men who rode past the Hite house while Frank and Jesse James waited at the windows, weapons ready. But Overton was well outside his North Alabama jurisdiction and applied to the local sheriff to make the arrests.

Scene 3

Curtain opens.

[The living room of the Donnie Pence house. Jesse and Zee James are hugging as Frank James, Dick Liddil and Clarence Hite enter. The children are clustered around their mother.]

Jesse: Zee, it is sure good to see you.

Zee: I was worried about you. Has anything happened?

Jesse: We had a little excitement but nothing serious.

Frank: We have decided that it is time we all went back to Missouri.

Jesse: Yeah, you and the kids can take the train on to Louisville. Clarence will escort you so that you should be safe. You can catch a train from Louisville to Kearney, Missouri from there. I will join you there as soon as I can. Probably in just a little while.

Zee: Are you sure? Do you think you will be safe?

Jesse: Sure, me and Dick will be right along. We will take the same route.

Frank: I will stay around here for a little while but I will join Annie and little Robert in Kansas City in a little while as well.

[At this point Zee, Clarence and the kids exit the stage.]

[Jesse then turns to Dick Liddil.]

Jesse: Dick, we will follow in about a week.

Dick: Jesse, our horses are plum wore out. They won't be any good much longer.

Jesse: We'll look around for now and steal some horses when we are ready.

Dick: Yeah, you always would rather ride a horse you stole than one of your own anyway! [both men chuckle.]

Jesse: It don't much matter to me as long as it will get me where I need to go! [Both men chuckle again.]

Frank: You men go on and plan that out. I'll stick around here for another week or more.

[Jesse and Dick exit the stage still chuckling leaving Frank standing alone in a state of depression.]

Frank James [talking half as if to himself and half as if praying]: My life has been upended overnight. Try as we might to break off our Bohemian life, things always occur to drive us back! It was a sense of despair brought on by that reckless Bill Ryan that drove us away from our little home–our happy little home– and again forced us to become a wanderer. [he intones sadly]

The curtain closes slowly.

Narration:

Everyone makes their way back to Missouri as planned. It was reputed that Zee rented a horse and buggy while in Louisville and sold them to two unsuspecting gentlemen before boarding the cars. This seems to be an audacious action for someone trying to flee and remain unnoticed but who knows. These folks were always looking for an opportunity to help themselves and were not the kind of people that you would expect to run into at church on Sunday!

Things started to unravel for the James brothers as soon as they returned to Missouri. Jesse was shot and killed by Bob and Charlie Ford at home in St. Joseph, Missouri on April 3, 1882, just a little over a year after the Muscle Shoals, Alabama payroll robbery.

Setting: The office of Thomas T. Crittenden, the Governor of Missouri.

Scene 4: Governor Crittenden's Office

Curtain opens.

[Governor Crittenden is busy shuffling through papers on his desk. There is a loud knock on the door.]

Crittenden: Come in.

Frank James: [enters the stage dressed smartly and wearing a black hat] He removes his holster and gun and places them on Governor Crittenden's desk and then removes his hat.] Governor, as I promised you, I am surrendering to you.

Crittenden [still sitting]: Good. I am sure that things will work out for you.

Frank James [motioning to his gun and belt]: I want you to know that I have not let another man touch my guns since 1861.

Crittenden: That may go good for you in your trial. You know that we are going to have to send you down to Gallatin, Missouri, to stand trial for the July 15, 1881 robbery of the Rock Island Railroad near Winston. The engineer and a passenger were killed there.

Frank James: I expected that. All that I ask for is a fair trial.

Crittenden: A fair trial you will have, I can guarantee that.

Frank James: I also don't want you to send me back up to Northfield, Minnesota. Those folks are still looking for me up there.

Crittenden: That I can't guarantee. I will have to think about that.

[Both men shake hands with Crittenden still sitting.]

Crittenden: Frank, you know this is the end of the James Gang. Everyone except you has either been killed or imprisoned. You were the last one and now you have surrendered.

Frank James: I know. You will probably celebrate tonight with a good meal while I am spending my first night in jail!

Curtain closes.

<u>INTERMISSION IF DESIRED</u>

Act 5 - Trial

Characters: Frank James, Huntsville Jailer, two Huntsville visitors, Judge Harry Bruce, District Attorney William H. Smith, former Assistant District Attorney Captain Lionel W. Day, Leroy Pope Walker, R. W. Walker, Raymond B. Sloan, James W. Newman, Bailiff, Madison County Sheriff, Thomas Peden, Alexander G. Smith, Dick Liddil, Silas Norris, Sarah Hite, Hugh Riley, Alfred G. Hill, Sam Fields, Justice of the Peace Bailey Brown, Jonas Taylor, W. H. Spann, Jack Smith, J. W. Davis, Mrs. E. A. Jones, Nashville newspaper reporter, friend of Annie James, Jury foreman.

Narration:

In the Deep South, six hundred miles away from Frank James' problems in Missouri, there was yet an old score to be settled. Someone had to pay society for the $5200 Muscle Shoals payroll robbery. And since Jesse was dead and "Wild Bill" Ryan was already serving a twenty-five year sentence, Alabama authorities were sure that the notorious Frank James was their man.

The Gallatin, Missouri trial was held in July, 1883 and Frank James was found not guilty.

Thus, although freed in Missouri, he was refused bail by United States Judge Judy Krekel and in February, 1884, the unhappy gunman was hustled aboard a train, and under guard, taken to Huntsville, Alabama.

Scene 1

Setting: Huntsville Jail

Setting: Frank James in a Huntsville jail cell awaiting trial wearing street clothes.

Curtain opens.

[Frank James is behind bars. The Jailer approaches the cell bringing fruit for Frank.]

Jailer: Here is some more fruit from your friends. They send you something every day, flowers and fruit, and visit you almost as often.

Frank James: I am truly blessed to have so many friends that I did not know before.

Jailer: Who was that person who gave you that gold ring the other day?

Frank: Another friend. They said they were an admirer of mine.

Jailer: And that fine suit for your trial - and the money that was sent to you from Missouri - I can't imagine anyone who would do that for you! Especially you!

Frank James: Again, I am truly blessed.

Jailer: I just can't understand all of this.

Frank James: What I can't understand is why I am being held in this filthy, flea ridden jail so long before they even read the charges against me. What is the problem down here anyway? I have been here since February! It is time to let he who is without sin cast the first stone!

[Frank then takes the fruit through the jail cell bars and returns some books to the jailer.]

Frank James: I am finished with these books. Can you bring me some others? About all that I care to read anymore is Shakespeare and the Bible. Can you bring me some more Shakespeare? Can you bring me some paper and a pencil? I would like to write to my wife.

Jailer: I will see what I can do. By the way, you have some more people out front who came to visit. I will get them now.

[The jailer exits and shortly brings back two men about Frank's age who visit him from through the jail cell bars.]

Frank James: Good morning, gentlemen. Just who do I thank for this nice visit?

First visitor: Me, I am Frank like you [then motioning to the other visitor] and this is Joe. We are old Confederates like you but we fought back east, not in the west like you.

Frank James: No matter where we fought, camp life and the fighting was pretty much the same. We all rallied around the "Old Stars and Bars" in those daring days!

First visitor: We sure did! That's true. We just wanted to drop by and try to keep your spirits up. You have been in here so long.

Frank James: Thanks for coming by and visiting for a while. You don't know how much it means to me to know that I am not forgotten - just sitting here alone in this privy of a jail and just rotting away forgotten. I guess that you folks have plenty of other things that you should be doing right now.

First visitor: Not much. It's too wet to get out an do much jist now.

[All three men shake hands and the visitors turn to exit.]

Curtain closes.

Narration:

Not until Wednesday April 16, 1884 did District Attorney L. W. Day read the indictment against Frank James before United States Circuit Court and twenty-odd government witnesses from the Muscle Shoals vicinity came forth to testify.

Judge Harry Bruce was impartially presiding. The prosecution Attorneys were United States District Attorney William H. Smith, former Reconstruction governor of Alabama, was chief prosecutor. He was assisted by Captain Lionel W. Day, former Assistant District Attorney.

The defense was led by General Leroy Pope Walker of Huntsville, formerly Confederate Secretary of War, as chief counsel. He was assisted by Raymond B. Sloan of Nashville, Tennessee and Richard W. Walker of Huntsville, and James W. Newman of Winchester, Tennessee.

It is speculated that their fees were probably paid by a Confederate veteran organization. The Federal Government paid the expenses of witnesses for the defense because Frank James claimed he was unable to do so.

The only woman in the courtroom the whole trial, except for a few witnesses, was the beautiful Annie Ralston James, the twenty seven year old wife of Frank, who was accompanied by their well-mannered six-year-old son Robert Frank. They sat quietly in the courtroom enlisting public sympathy by their genteel appearance and circumspect demeanor.

We will now dispense with normal court protocol and dwell mostly on the testimony of the witnesses. The Judge, Prosecuting Attorneys and the Defense Attorneys as well as Frank James will remain on stage while the witnesses will give their testimony to the Jury - [motioning to the entire audience] and you will sit in for the jury for this trial. Listen carefully to the testimony and make up your mind based strictly on the testimony.

The first day of the trial preliminaries on Wednesday April 16, 1884 went pretty much like this.

Scene 2

Setting: First day of trial preliminaries in Judge Harry Bruce's court room. The prosecution team is seated at one table and the defense team with Frank James is seated at the other. Annie and little Robert James are seated in chairs off to one side of the stage.

Curtain opens.

Judge Harry Bruce [beats his gavel]: This court is now in session. Will the people now read the indictment?

Mr. Day [arises and reads]: The Grand Jurors of the United States. . For the body of said northern district of Alabama upon their oaths present that heretofore and to wit, on the Eleventh day of March A. D. 1881, in said northern district of Alabama, in the county of Lauderdale, Jesse James, Frank James, Thomas Hill alias William Ryan alias Dick Ryan and Richard Little, alias Dick Little, alias Dick Liddil, alias Richard Lee, unlawfully and fraudulently conspired, combined, confederated and agreed together between themselves and with diverse other evil disposed persons of the Grand Jurors unknown, to rob one Alexander G. Smith of a large sum of money…

They, with force of arms, made an assault upon the said Alexander G. Smith and then and therefore feloniously and violently took from the person of the said Alexander G. Smith against his will, and carried away, the said sum…

Judge Bruce: How does the defendant plead?

Frank James [arises]: Not guilty, your Honor.

Judge Bruce: Are the people ready?

Mr. Day [arises again]: We are not, your honor. Two of our witnesses are not present.

Judge Bruce: This trial is postponed until 9:00 AM tomorrow. [beats his gavel]

[Everyone remains seated on stage.]

Narration:

The two witnesses that were not present were Mrs. Sarah Hite and Mr. Silas Norris, two important witnesses for the prosecution. The Marshal of the Nashville District had telegraphed that the two were not in Nashville, they had left for Hendersonville the night before.

The next morning April 17, 1884 both sides were ready to begin the trial. Remember we are only dealing primarily with the testimony of the witnesses and not established court protocol.

All morning was spent selecting a jury. General Walker and Governor Smith immediately plunged into quarrels over legal technicalities, much to the delight of the spectators. The selection of the jury went quickly though and all twelve jurymen were seated in the morning. A reporter described them as "a very fair looking body, most of them evidently from the country."

The weather that April was wet, too wet for planting, and farmers from the Huntsville-Madison County area flocked into town to watch the trial and catch a glimpse of the famous outlaw.

Setting: Judge Harry Bruce's Courtroom

Scene 3

Judge Bruce [beating his gavel]: This court is now in session. Are the people ready?

Governor Smith [rises]: We are your Honor.

Judge Bruce: Is the defense ready?

Leroy Walker [rises]: We are, your Honor.

Judge Bruce: The people may present their case. It is the responsibility of the prosecution to prove their case to the jury beyond any shadow of doubt.

Governor Smith [rising and facing the Judge]: Thank you, your honor. We understand.

[Facing the audience] It is well known that the James-Younger Gang and later the James Gang were murderous, violent and brutal bands of outlaws. The man before you today accused of the crimes specified in the indictment [pointing toward Frank James] was a member of both cold-blooded groups. The men belonging to these gangs were indiscriminate killers, robbers and they thought nothing of committing their evil deeds upon society at large.

The people will prove, by testimony of reliable witnesses that they witnessed, first hand, that the accused was indeed in the Shoals area on March 11, 1881, and by Alexander Smith, who was robbed, that Frank James was indeed not only one of the men who committed the robbery, but was indeed the ring leader of the group!

Judge Bruce: The people can call their first witness.

Governor Smith: The people call Thomas Peden.

[Thomas Peden enters the witness stand.]

[The Bailiff is standing in front of the witness stand.]

Bailiff: What is your name?

Peden: Thomas Peden.

Bailiff: Place your right hand on the Bible. Do you swear that the testimony you give will be the truth, the whole truth, and nothing but the truth, so help you God?

Thomas Peden: I do.

Bailiff: You may be seated. [and retires to the other side of the bench.]

Gov. Smith [approaches the bench]: Mr. Peden, do you own a saloon near Lock Three of the Muscle Shoals canal?

Peden: I do.

Smith: And can you tell us in your own words what happened the morning of April 11, 1881 at your saloon.

Peden: There are a lot of people who come to see the construction of the canal project. A lot of them visit my saloon. On the day of the robbery, three strangers who caught my attention, visited my saloon at lunchtime. They hitched their horses under a shade tree and came inside. One man had black whiskers and was tolerably well dressed. The other two were lighter. They had a couple of drinks and two of them walked out. The third settled the bill.

I then sat on a lumber pile outside with one of the men, talking. The man wanted to talk about the canal. He also talked about politics. The man also wanted to know about how the Negroes were doing. Had slaves been hard to manage?

After a while the men ate cheese and crackers and rode off to the east. Two of the riders went out first. The third followed 100 to 130 yards behind on a sorrel **with a peculiar lump on its back.**

Gov. Smith: Was Frank James one of these men?

Peden: Yes, he was.

Governor Smith: That is all, your Honor.

General Walker [approaching the witness]: Mr. Peden. Are you sure that you knew for certain that Frank James was one of these men? Don't you remember that you were taken into the Huntsville jail before the trial and Frank James was pointed out to you?

Peden: Well ...

General Walker: Are you absolutely sure that you remember Frank James being one of these men?

Peden: Well...

General Walker: To help you be absolutely sure we will have the Sheriff put a hat on Frank James and let you look at him. [Turning toward the Sheriff] Sheriff, please put a slouch hat on Frank James and let Mr. Peden get a good look at him.

[Madison County Sheriff puts a slouch hat similar to the ones the robbers had worn that day on Frank James and Frank then walks back and forth in front of Thomas Peden.]

General Walker: Are you positively and absolutely sure that this man, Frank James, was one of the men at your saloon the day of the robbery?

179

Peden: Well…he resembles one of the men that was in my saloon that day.

But under oath, I cannot say for sure he is one of the men. He resembles one of the men, but I cannot say for certain that he was one of the men. [Turning to address Frank James] Mr. James, if you did the robbery you ought to be punished. I'd say that your nose and forehead look the same, but I shan't say that you are the man.

Judge Bruce: That is all. Mr. Peden, you are excused. [Thomas Peden Exit's the stage.]

Gov. Smith: For my next witness I call Mr. Alexander G. Smith.

[Smith enters the witness stand.]

Judge Bruce: Mr. Smith, you are already sworn in.

Gov Smith [approaching the witness]: Mr. Smith, tell us in your own words what happened to you in the afternoon of April 11, 1881.

Alexander Smith: I was carrying $5200 that day to pay off the men working on the canal. Five hundred dollars was in gold, $500 was in silver and the rest was in paper. I was the timekeeper of the project and the engineer had sent me to Florence to pick up the money. On the way back, I passed three riders. As I neared the canal, about four miles east of Peden's place, I heard a noise and three men stuck pistols to my head. I dismounted in the bed of the canal which had not been filled with water, and the men searched my pockets and my saddlebags.

The men then ordered me to come with them. One man rode ahead and one to his side. The other rode behind. After we had been riding six or seven miles, the men divided the money. They kept me in the woods until dark. The men said we were on the edge of Tennessee. The last I saw of the men they were riding north toward Nashville.

Gov. Smith: Your witness, Mr. Walker.

General Walker [approaching the witness]: Mr. Smith, I understand that you traveled to Nashville and positively identified William Ryan as one to the robbers.

Alexander Smith: Yes, I did.

General Walker: Can you with equal certainty identify Frank James as also being one of the robbers? With absolute certainty under oath? Take a good look at him.

Alexander Smith: I think that Frank James was one of the men, I believe that he was, but I cannot say he was positively one of them.

Judge Bruce: You are excused Mr. Smith.

[Alexander Smith exits the stage]

Judge Bruce [banging his gavel]: The court will break for the day at this point. We will reconvene at 9 AM Friday April 18, 1884.

Narration:

The testimony of J. N. Wilcoxon ended this day of the trial. He testified that he met three men the day of the robbery but his description differed from that of Thomas Peden. The prosecution had a bombshell ready for the opening day Friday April 18 and they were ready to unleash it on the defense.

Judge Bruce [banging his gavel]: This court is now in session.

Governor Smith: The people call as their next witness James Andrew Liddil.

General Walker [arises quickly]: I object your Honor. This man is an incompetent witness! He has been convicted of stealing a mare valued at $50 in Vernon County, Missouri in 1874.

Governor Smith: Mr. Liddil has been pardoned for that offense. The people would like to enter into evidence a copy of his pardon [holding it aloft and approaching the bench.]

Judge Bruce: The objection is overruled. The pardon will be entered into evidence. The testimony of this witness is allowed.

Governor Smith: Thank you, your Honor.

[Dick Liddil enters the witness stand.]

Judge Bruce: You are already sworn in Mr. Liddil.

Governor Smith: Tell us in your own words just how you came to know Frank James.

Dick Liddil: I first met Frank and Jesse James about twelve years ago at their headquarters in Jackson County, Missouri. I was honestly employed at work there but I soon joined their group for several years. When Frank and Jesse moved to Tennessee, I followed them, and for a time I lived in and about Nashville with Jim Cummins, Ed Miller and other members of the gang.

One night, Jim Cummins suddenly disappeared. The rest of us feared that he intended to betray us so we scattered the better to hide.

Governor Smith: Thank you Mr. Liddil. Will you now tell us what happened before the Muscle Shoals robbery?

Dick Liddil: Frank, Jesse and "Wild Bill" set out on March 6 toward the south intendin' to arrange for a train robbery later in the spring and mark out a line of retreat. Upon Frank and Jesse's advice, I set out for Adairsville, Logan County, Kentucky, just across the Tennessee border, about forty miles due north of Nashville. There I was to stay with our friends George T. Hite and his sons Robert Woodson Hite, alias Wood Hite and Old Grimes, and Clarence Browler Hite, favorite first cousins of Frank and Jesse and sometimes gang members.

But like I said before, in March 6, Jesse and Ryan moved out before daylight and Frank followed about 7 o'clock. They didn't say where they were goin'.

In Nashville, Frank was known as B. J. Woodson, Jesse was J. D. Howard, Ryan was Thomas Hill and I was Joe Smith.

When they left, Frank and Jesse had sandy beards. **Frank was riding a sorrel horse with roan hair. It had a small scar on its forehead and it had a lump on its back.** Frank had brought a gray horse for Ryan, who had a black beard. Jesse was on a brown horse.

Governor Smith: Thank You, Mr. Liddil. Can you tell the court what happened next?

Dick Liddil: When they came back, the James boys wore moustaches and burnsides. Ryan had only a moustache. When they came back the gang stayed in Nashville for a couple of days. Then Ryan got a few miles out of town and got to drinking. He made the mistake of pulling a pistol on a justice of the peace. He was arrested. The James boys and I went on to stay with friends in Logan County, Kentucky, the day after he was arrested.

Governor Smith: Thank you, Mr. Liddil. That is all for the people.

General Walker: I have no questions for this witness just now but I may want to recall him later.

[Dick Liddil exits the stage.]

Governor Smith: The people call Mr. Silas Norris to the stand.

[Mr. Norris enters the witness stand.]

Judge Bruce: You are already sworn in Mr. Norris.

Governor Smith: Mr. Norris, Did you see Frank James in March of 1881?

Mr. Norris: Yes I did. He and Dick Liddil spent several days with us at the Hite place in Adairsville, Kentucky.

Governor Smith: Thank you, Mr. Norris. You are excused.

[Silas Norris exits the stage.]

Governor Smith: The People call Mrs. Robert Woodson Hite to the stand.

[Mrs. Hite enters the witness stand.]

Judge Bruce: You have already been sworn in Mrs. Hite.

Gov. Smith: Mrs. Hite will you tell the court if you saw Frank James at your home in March 1881?

Mrs. Hite: Yes, I did. He and Dick Liddil spent several days with us there. But Frank James was never at our house but that one time. Other members of the James gang visited us quite regular.

Governor Smith: Thank you, Mrs. Hite. That is all.

[Mrs. Hite exits the stage.]

Judge Bruce [banging his gavel]: Court is adjourned at this point until tomorrow at 9 AM which is Saturday April 19, 1884.

Narration:

This ended the session on Friday April 18. The prosecution has almost completed their arguments and the defense will start tomorrow. Who knows what they will have to say? This should be exciting! All of the residents in the Huntsville-Madison County think so. They pack the courtroom to overflowing each day, even congregating in the halls.

Judge Bruce [banging his gavel:] This court is now in session.

Mr. Day: The people now call Mr. Hugh Riley to the stand.

[Hugh Riley enters the witness stand.]

Judge Bruce: You have already been sworn in Mr. Riley.

Mr. Day: Mr. Riley, will you tell the court, in your own words, just what you saw in Mr. Peden's saloon the morning of April 11, 1881?

Mr. Riley: Well, these three strangers came in the saloon 'bout noon and ordered a couple of drinks and some cheese and crackers. They didn't do nothing out of the ordinary. They then went outside and one of them sat on a lumber pile talkin' with Mr. Peden for awhile and then left. We didn't know they were outlaws at that time. We didn't hear nothing' bout the robbery until the next day. We figgered they must have been the robbers.

Mr. Day: Is one of the men present in the courtroom?

Hugh Riley [pointing to Frank James]: That feller over there looks similar to one of the men. [He takes a longer look at Frank] But it's been a good three years and I can't say for sure.

Mr. Day: Are you positive about that?

Hugh Riley: No, I can't say for sure that he was one of them.

[Day throws up his hands in disbelief and walks back to the prosecution table.]

Judge Bruce: That is all Mr. Riley. You may be excused.

[Hugh Riley exits the stage.]

Mr. Day: The people call Mr. Alfred G. Hill to the stand.

[Alfred Hill enters the witness stand.]

Judge Bruce: You have already been sworn in Mr. Hill.

Mr. Day: Mr. Hill, tell the court, in your own words, just what happened at your house just before the March 11, 1881 robbery?

Alfred Hill: These three men come up to my house in Atlas just north of the canal works and wanted to spend the night at my house, which they did as I take in a few boarders from time to time. They were very interested in the canal works, like they wanted to know when the workers were paid. I thought at first they might be looking for work. But they said that two of them were revenue agents and the other was a fruit tree peddler. I ask the one feller about what kind of fruit trees he had, but he didn't have none with him.

Mr. Day: Mr. Hill, is one of the men in the courtroom today?

Alfred Hill: [looks toward Frank James]: That feller over there looks a little bit like one of them.

Mr. Day: Take a good look at him Mr. Hill. Was he one of the men?

Alfred Hill: [after looking at Frank James a little longer]: Like I said he looks a little bit like one of them, but I can't say for sure!

Mr. Day: Mr. Hill, are you positive he is not one of the men?

Alfred Hill: Like I said, I can't be sure.

[Day throws up his hands in disbelief again but stomps back to the prosecution table this time.]

Judge Bruce: That is all Mr. Hill. You can step down now.

Governor Smith [standing]: The prosecution rests.

Judge Bruce: The defense can begin.

R. W. Walker [facing the audience]: We compliment the district attorney's masterly presentation of the law and evidence on his side!

We intend to show that Frank James did not take any part in the Muscle Shoals robbery. He was not even in Muscle Shoals at this time. He was in Nashville, Tennessee as the following fine and upstanding witnesses will testify. These witnesses will show by their testimony that Frank James lived in Nashville as a hard working steady citizen from 1877 until April 16, 1881. [turning to the judge] We call as our first witness Mr. Sam Fields of Nashville, Tennessee.

[Sam Fields enters the witness stand.]

Judge Bruce: You are already sworn in Mr. Fields.

R. W. Walker: Just what do you do in Nashville, Mr. Fields?

Sam Fields: I am a detective:

R. W. Walker: And Mr. Fields, just how did you get to know Ben Woodson or Frank James?

Sam Fields: I have known Frank James, as Ben Woodson, since 1879. I didn't know until later that he was Frank James. Frank was hauling hogs for the Indiana Lumber Company, which is located on the river east of Nashville.

R. W. Walker: Thank you, Mr. Fields. Did you see Frank James the day of April 11, 1881?

Sam Fields: Yes, Frank was in Nashville that day. I know it was that day because a particular case, Stephens vs. Chickering, was being heard that day by Justice of the Peace Bailey Brown. Frank, I, Dave Pitman and Theodore Willard walked up Cherry Street after the hearing. I also saw him at Jonas Taylor's shop and saw him in front of Fisher's saloon.

R. W. Walker: Thank you, Mr. Fields. You may step down now.

[Sam Fields exits the stage.]

R. W. Walker: We call as our next witness Jonas Taylor.

[Jonas Taylor enters the witness stand.]

Judge Bruce: You have already been sworn in Mr. Taylor.

R. W. Walker: And just how did you get to know Frank James Mr. Taylor?

Jonas Taylor: I met Ben Woodson in Nashville in 1878. We were introduced by Berry Cheatham. Woodson lived on the Drake place in White's Creek, and later on the Smith place and he later moved nearer town. J. D. Howard owned two race horses in partnership with me. They were named Jim Malone and Col. Hull. We bought them on credit from Jim Malone and Morris Landers. We raced the horses at fairs.

R. W. Walker: Thank you, Mr. Taylor. Did you see Frank James on April 11, 1881?

Jonas Taylor: Yes, I did. He was at the shop on April 11th and 12th. [holding up a couple of well worn bound ledgers] Here are my books to prove that Woodson was in my shop those days.

I saw him again five or ten days later. He dropped by to say goodbye. He said he was goin' to Florida. Jesse kept a boarding house near the race track.

R. W. Walker [taking the ledgers and approaching the bar]: We would like to submit these ledgers into evidence.

Judge Bruce: So ordered.   [banging his gavel] This is a good place to break for today. We will resume at 9:00 AM Monday April 21.

Narration:

Things are beginning to heat up now aren't they? They will get hotter before the trial is over.

One thing that Alfred Hill did not mention in his testimony, he was married to Sarah C. James at the time of the robbery. The James boys had a habit of visiting with friends and relatives. Could there be a connection? The local Rogers and Gray families think so. They have long claimed that Joshua James, Sarah's father, was the uncle of Frank and Jesse James.

Anyway, by Saturday, public sentiment in Huntsville was running strongly in favor of Frank James. The trial was the only subject of discussion among the customary Saturday visitors to town. A reporter observed that the people gather in knots on the corners and argue legal points as if they held a connection with the counsel in the case.

This is basically what transpired on Monday April 21:

Judge Bruce [banging his gavel]: This court is now in session.

[Jonas Taylor is still in the witness box.]

Gov. Smith: Your honor, we have examined these ledgers and would like to point out several inconsistencies.

First, there are differences in the handwriting in which the entries are made.

Secondly, the entries for April 11 and 12 are not made in the same columns as previous entries.

Thirdly, the ledgers are mutilated and smeared.

R. W. Walker: Mr. Taylor, can you explain this?

Jonas Taylor: I cannot write so my books are kept for me by friends. These particular accounts have been in a fire since 1881.

R. W. Walker: Thank you, Mr. Taylor. That is all. You may step down now.

[Jonas Taylor exits the stage.]

R. W. Walker: We would like to call co-council R. B. Sloan to the stand next.

[Sloan enters the witness stand.]

Judge Bruce: You are already sworn in Mr. Sloan.

R. W. Walker: Mr. Sloan, can you tell the court exactly what you know about these ledgers?

Sloan: These books are in the same condition that they were in when I first saw them when I was investigating James on a case in Gallatin, Missouri. I knew Woodson slightly in Nashville. J. B. Howard had a celebrated race horse named Jim Malone. I never saw Woodson and Howard together. As for the boarding house, when I knew about it, it was operated by a Mrs. Snowden, and it was a house of bad repute. The court had to take it over and rented it to laborers.

R. W. Walker: Thank you Mr. Sloan, you may step down now.

[Sloan returns to the defense table and sits down.]

R. W. Walker: For our next witness, we would like to call Justice of the Peace J. Bailey Brown.

[Bailey Brown enters the witness stand.]

Judge Bruce: You have already been sworn in Mr. Brown.

R. W. Walker: Mr. Brown, I see you have brought your books with you. What do they show?

Bailey Brown [opening his books]: It shows here that Stephens vs. Chickering was tried before me on April 11th and 12th of 1881.

R. W. Walker [taking the books and approaching the bench]: Your honor, we would like to enter these ledgers into evidence.

Judge Bruce: So ordered.

R. W. Walker: Thank you, Mr. Brown. You may step down now.

[Bailey Brown exits the stage.]

R. W. Walker: We would like to call W. H. Spann to the stand next.

[W. H. Spann enters the witness stand.]

Judge Bruce: You have already been sworn in Mr. Spann.

R. W. Walker: Mr. Spann, just how did you know Ben Woodson?

Mr. Spann: I knew Ben Woodson when he lived on the Hyde's Ferry Place and later when he lived in Edgemont in East Nashville.

In 1880, he lived on the Jeff Hyde place a quarter of a mile from me. I saw him often in '80 and early '81. He farmed and later hauled hogs. I was driving his mules and wagon in February with my brother in-law's horse tied behind when I was in a ferry accident. The horse and the rear of the wagon was lost. I saw him on the square in Nashville on the 11th about sending out new wheels. He lived in Edgemont then. I saw him on the 12th to talk about the pedigree of some hogs I bought from George Harvey.

R. W. Walker: Thank you, Mr. Spann. You may step down now.

[Mr. Spann exits the stage.]

R. W. Walker: We would like to call Mr. Robert Dale next.

[Robert Dale enters the witness stand.]

Judge Bruce: You have already been sworn in Mr. Dale.

R. W. Walker: Mr. Dale, how did you know Ben Woodson?

Robert Dale: I am W. H. Spann's brother in-law and I run a grocery store and live next to the Jeff Hyde place. I was a neighbor of Ben Woodson.

R. W. Walker: Do you know anything about the wagon accident?

Robert Dale: I sure do. I lost a good horse in that accident. A very good horse!

R. W. Walker: Thank you, Mr. Dale. You may step down.

[Robert Dale exits the stage]

R. W. Walker: We call Mr. Jack Smith next.

[Jack Smith, a Negro, enters the witness stand.]

Judge Bruce: You have already been sworn in Mr. Smith.

R. W. Walker: Mr. Smith, what is your occupation?

Jack Smith: I am a railroad detective for Major Geddes.

R. W. Walker: Mr. Smith, did you know Ben Woodson?

Jack Smith: I sure did.

R. W. Walker: Did you see Mr. Woodson on April 11, 1881?

Jack Smith: I did. I saw him on Deadrick Street the day of the robbery and saw him on the corner of College and Union the next day.

R. W. Walker: Thank you, Mr. Smith. You can step down now.

[Jack Smith exits the stage.]

Judge Bruce: We will take a break here. Court will reconvene tomorrow, Tuesday April 22, 1884 at 9 AM.

[Everyone files off stage.]

Curtain.

Narration:

All of the surprises have not been sprung yet.

General Walker was ill on Tuesday and the trial was postponed until Wednesday April 23rd.

An unknown reporter from Nashville interviewed a friend of Annie James and then Frank James on Tuesday while there was a break in the trial. This account was published in the February 28, 1971 The Nashville Tennessean Magazine.

Scene 4

Setting: A table on one side of the stage where the reporter and the friend are sitting with Frank James jail cell on the other.

Curtain opens.

Reporter: I understand that you are good friends with Mrs. James and that you have spoken with her recently. Is this true?

Female friend: Yes, I have.

Reporter: How is Mrs. James holding up through all of this?

Female friend: She is holding up quite well. She is such a cheerful person and is so confident. I fear that should the verdict be anything but acquittal that it will kill her.

Reporter: I fear that is true. Thank you. [The reporter gets up from the table and walks over to Frank James' jail cell. Frank is behind cell bars and the reporter is interviewing him from the other side of the bars.]

Reporter: Mr. James, I wanted to take this time with you to discuss a rumor that is going around that you are going to get Dick Liddil when you are freed.

Frank James: Dick Liddil has nothing to fear from me. I try not to think of him. When I recall what he has done to me, it makes me feel fearful. Why, I wouldn't even dirty my hands with him. If he had any manhood whatever, he would go hang himself, like Judas.

Reporter: I hear that you have received threatening letters.

Frank James: I did receive a postcard with a Nashville postmark. It had a drawing of a gallows and a skull and crossbones. It said that if the jury in Huntsville don't hang you, you will not escape us. It was signed Ford Brothers. [Frank hands it through the cell bars for the reporter to examine.]

Reporter: I figure this is a prank.

Frank James: I think so too.

[Frank James holds out his hands toward the reporter] My hands don't much look like they could handle a plow and a hoe now, but they will get used to it again!

Curtain closes.

Narration:

The happening on Wednesday April 23rd was a barnburner. The defense uncorked a tempest that may have sealed the outcome of the trial.

All of the testimony this day is not given here, only that which most directly affected the outcome of the trial.

Scene 5

Setting: Judge Harry Bruce's courtroom

Curtain opens.

[Judge Bruce and the prosecution as well at the defense team with Mrs. James and little Robert are seated.]

Judge Bruce [banging his gavel]: This court is now in session.

Mr. Day [rises]: Your honor, the people would like to call two more witnesses for the people.

Judge Bruce: Granted.

Mr. Day: The people would like to call J. W Davis.

[J. W. Davis enters the witness stand.]

Judge Bruce: You are already sworn in Mr. Davis.

Mr. Day: Mr. Davis, did you see the three strangers the day of April 11, 1881?

Davis: I did. I live about ten miles west of Florence and that day I was visiting to check out the progress of the canal. I was at Peden's saloon when they came in. They looked pretty much like Mr. Peden and Hugh Riley said.

Mr. Day: Mr. Davis, do you see one of the men in the courtroom?

Mr. Davis: That man over there [pointing to Frank James] looks familiar.

Mr. Day: Can you absolutely say that he was one of the men?

Mr. Davis: He does look familiar but I can't say that he was.

Mr. Day: Are you absolutely sure of that?

Mr. Davis: No, I can't say that he absolutely was.

[Day shakes his head not believing what he has heard and walks back to the prosecution table.]

Judge Bruce: Thank you Mr. Davis. You may step down now.

[J. W. Davis exits the stage.]

Mr. Day: The people call Mrs. E. A. Jones next.

[Mrs. Jones enters the witness stand.]

Judge Bruce: You have already been sworn in Mrs. Jones.

Mr. Day: Mrs. Jones, can you tell the court where you live?

Mrs. Jones: I live in Columbia, Tennessee now but I lived in Laurel Hill, Tennessee in 1881.

Mr. Day: Mrs. Jones, can you tell the court what happened at your house just before April 11, 1881?

Mrs. Jones: Three men came by my house two or three days before the robbery and asked to spend the night. They left after breakfast the next morning but they wanted to know the way to Muscle Shoals before they left.

Mr. Day: Mrs. Jones, do you see one of these men in the courtroom today?

Mrs. Jones [pointing to Frank James]: He may have been, but I don't know.

Mr. Day: Mrs. Jones, are you sure of that?

Mrs. Jones: Yes, I don't think that he was.

[Day throws up his hands again in desperation and stomps back to the prosecution table.]

Judge Bruce: You may step down now Mrs. Jones.

[Mrs. Jones exits the stage.]

Mr. James W. Newman [rising]: Your Honor, the Defense would like to recall Mr. Richard Liddil at this time.

[Dick Liddil enters the witness stand.]

Judge Bruce: You are already sworn in Mr. Liddil.

Mr. Newman [Pointing a finger at Dick Liddil and sneering]: Mr. Liddil, Why do you need so many aliases? Could it be because of your cold-blooded treacheries and traitorous actions against your friends and because of your dishonest thievery?

Dick Liddil: I thought that I needed them at the time.

Mr. Newman: Mr. Liddil, is it not true that you have been a horse thief, a train robber and a murderer?

Dick Liddil: I have been a horse thief and have been convicted of several other offenses and have served time in the Missouri penitentiary for them.

Mr. Newman: Is it not also true that you have five more indictments pending against you in Missouri?

Dick Liddil: That is true, I do have other indictments against me in Missouri.

Mr. Newman: Is it not also true that you have been promised immunity for these indictments if you testify against Frank James in this trial?

Dick Liddil: I have been brought to Alabama to testify against Frank, under agreement with Missouri authorities that their influence will be used to relieve me of future prosecution and penalties for each and all offenses charged against me.

Mr. Newman: If this witness before you [he shouts facing the audience] had been at Bosworth field when Richard III cried "A horse! A horse! My kingdom for a horse!" Dick Liddil would have said, "Don't be troubled oh King! I will steal one for you in just a minute!" [Newman turns and stomps back to the defense table.]

Judge Bruce: Mr. Liddil, that is all. You may step down.

[Dick Liddil exits the stage.]

Judge Bruce [banging his gavel]: We will break for the day at this point. Court will reconvene tomorrow Thursday April 24, 1884 at 9 AM.

Narration:

Wasn't Dick Liddil's testimony a surprise? But we still have two more days before the jury reaches its verdict. Anything can, and probably will, happen before that!

Sentiments in Huntsville were even more favorable to Frank James than when the trial began. A reporter commented that on the streets nothing but the most ardent wishes for his acquittal are heard.

The closing arguments for both parties were heard Thursday April 24th.

Judge Bruce [beating his gavel]: This court is now in session for closing arguments.

Governor Smith [standing and facing the audience]: The people have proven, by testimony of reliable witnesses that they witnessed, first hand, that the accused, Frank James, was indeed in the Shoals area on March 11, 1881, and by Alexander Smith, who was robbed, that Frank James was indeed not only one of the men who committed the robbery, but was indeed the ring leader of the group!

The jury can reach no other verdict from the evidence presented that the accused is guilty of the crimes specified in the indictment and be found guilty of these crimes. [Returns to the prosecution table and sits down.]

Leroy Pope Walker [standing and facing the audience]: I am proud of the privilege of serving the defendant, former private Alexander Franklin James of the Confederate States Army, not only because I believe him innocent of all charges, but also because he was a Confederate – a man who bravely came to the aid of the South in its great hour of need. Alexander Franklin James, as a lad in his teens, enlisted in the Missouri State Guards, a Confederate regiment under the command of General Sterling Price. Frank fought fierce fights against the Yankees at the Battle of Wilson's Creek, near Springfield, Missouri on August 10, 1861, the first important clash of arms, save First Bull Run, in the War for Southern Independence. Frank was subsequently captured by the Federals, he was jailed and ultimately escaped to join Quantrill's Black Flag Brigade. He participated in the famous Lawrence, Kansas raid, and he fought an everlasting battle against Yankee Jayhawkers all across the length and breadth of the Missouri-Kansas border country, and his love for the Southland cannot be disputed.

[In low, whispered tones] The Yankee militia retaliated against Confederate Frank James by horse-whipping his fifteen-year-old brother Jesse and hanging his aged stepfather to a tree, while they tossed hand grenades into his home, setting it a-fire, blowing off his mother's right arm at the elbow and instantly killing his little half brother, Archie – all because they were Southern sympathizers. [He turns to Annie James and little Robert Frank in tearful tones] Look at Mrs. James and little Robert just sitting there with their gentility and poise. It would be nothing but the proper and right thing for you to do but grant freedom to their beloved husband and tender father, a gentleman wrongly accused and oft humiliated.

Judge Bruce [beating his gavel]: This court is now in recess until tomorrow Friday April 25, 1884 and we will resume at 9 AM.

Narration:

Everyone agreed that General Walker's defense was the "ablest of many able speeches" the great Confederate warrior and barrister had ever delivered and through it all, the *Democrat* added "Mr. And Mrs. James sat cool, calm and collected . . . Slight flushes playing now and then on their pale but unmoved faces."

Judge Harry Bruce gave the jury a "very clear, fair and impartial charge at 1:30 the afternoon of Friday April 25, 1884 and the twelve old Confederates, good men and true, filed out one after the other, slowly and solemnly. They returned at 6:30 PM with their verdict.

Judge Bruce [banging his gavel]: Has the jury reached its verdict?

Jury Foreman: We have your Honor.

Judge Bruce: What is your verdict?

Jury Foreman: We the jury find the defendant, Frank James–- Not Guilty!

Judge Bruce [beating his gavel, shouts]: **The defendant is discharged!**

[Frank James shakes the hands of his defense team. Other supporters pat Frank on the back.]

Narration:

Instantly, the crowd "loudly applauded" and shouts rang through the courtroom and down the hallways, for the verdict was "almost universally approved." The *Democrat* reporter added, however, that *he* thought such ungenteel enthusiasm "exceedingly wrong." A free man, Frank James rushed over and gratefully shook General Walker's hand. Admirers patted him on the back and Huntsville ladies gathered sympathetically about poor, weary Mrs. James and wide-eyed, innocent little Robert Frank James.

The Missouri officials were to keep jurisdiction over Frank James pending other charges against him there, but they never came to trial. They also kept him from being extradited to Minnesota.

Frank James lived as a law abiding citizen for thirty more years and died on February 18, 1915 in Independence, Missouri at age 72. He is buried next to Annie James in the Hill Park Cemetery.

Curtain closes.

Chapter 27

What Happened to Leroy Pope Walker and to the Outlaws?

Leroy Pope Walker died on August 24, 1884, four months to the day after he gave the closing arguments in the Huntsville, Alabama trial of Frank James, and is buried in lot 5 of the Maple Hill Cemetery in Huntsville, Alabama in his family plot. This is in the original two acres of Maple Hill Cemetery. As can be seen from the photograph below, there is a monument in the center of the plot. The inscription of this monument is in Latin and reads ORA PRO NOBIS. Family members are buried around the perimeter of the family plot.. The grave markers of some family members face north while others face south. Leroy Pope Walker's grave marker faces south.

Leroy Pope Walker's grave marker is shown below.

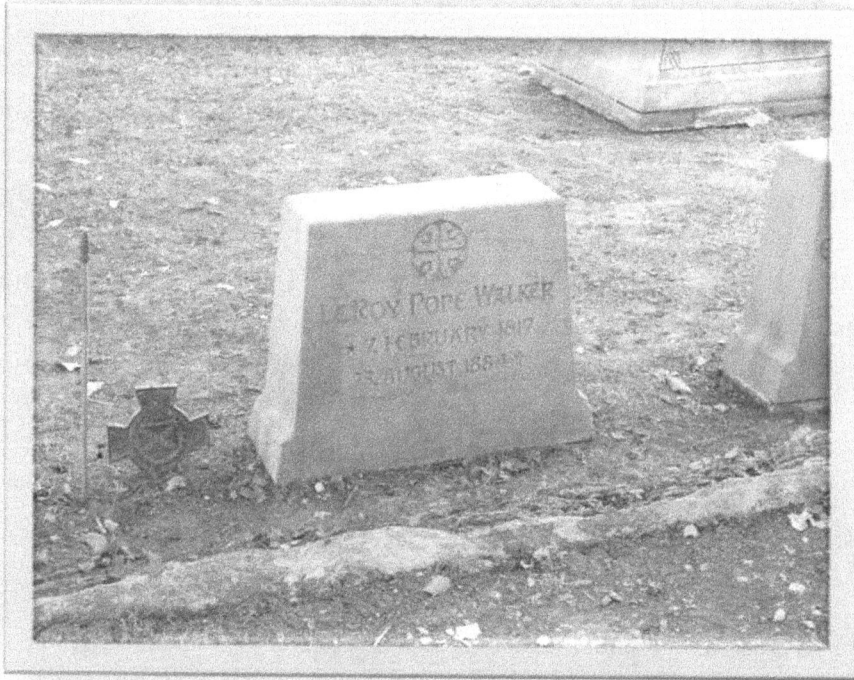

Photographs by Cindy and Dennis Liuzzo of Huntsville, Alabama in August 2010.

What happened to the outlaws mentioned in this book? The answer can be found on the internet on the website **James-Younger Gang: Outlaws**. This website is well worth reading in its entirety because many outlaws not mentioned in this work are listed there. The outlaws are listed in this work are in alphabetical order based on their last names.

1. Jim Cummins: James Robert Cummins, born January 31, 1847 in Missouri, son of Samuel and Eleanor Cummins. Jim rode with Quantrill and Anderson. He became a farmer in Arkansas. Married at age 63 to Florence Sherwood. Cummins lived in old age at the Old Soldiers Home in Higginsville, Missouri for 27 years. He died July 9, 1929. Jim Cummins tried to turn himself in several times after the James Gang broke up but no one believed he was really Jim Cummins so he was never tried for any crimes. In his book he seemed a bit disappointed about this. Jim wrote a book in 1902 about Quantrill and the James-Younger Gang.

No one in the band ever had much use for the little sniveler and cry-baby.

From other sources, Jim Cummins disappeared while living in the Nashville area and no one knew where he was. The gang members were fearful that he was planning to turn them in so they split up for awhile.

According to Dick Liddil's testimony and another source, Jesse James, getting more paranoid and suspicious all the time, tried to talk other gang members into having him killed but other gang members refused.

Robberies attributed to Jim Cummins:

None.

2. Bob Ford: Robert Newton Ford, son of Thomas Ford, born January 31, 1862. He killed Jesse James in 1882. He pleaded guilty to 1st degree murder, was sentenced to be hanged, but was quickly pardoned by the governor of Missouri. He was acquitted for the murder of Wood Hite. Bob Ford died violently in his Colorado bar on June 8, 1892, killed by Ed O. Kelly. The birth date shown on the tombstone as Bob Ford's is December 8, 1841 and is not correct.

3. Charlie Ford: Charles Wilson Ford, born July 9, 1857 participated in the killing of Jesse James. Pleaded guilty to 1st degree murder, sentenced to be hanged, but was quickly pardoned by the governor of Missouri. Charlie committed suicide on May 4, 1884. His age was given as 24 at the inquest into the death of Jesse James.

Robberies attributed to Charlie Ford:

- Blue Cut, train, Missouri September 1881.

4. Clarence Hite: Clarence Browler Hite born about 1862. Was the son of George B. and Nancy James Hite of Logan County Kentucky. Clarence was the first cousin of Frank and Jesse James. Arrested in Kentucky February 11, 1882 and taken to Missouri (with dubious attention paid to extradition laws and procedures). He was sentenced to 25 years for the Winston robbery, died of consumption in 1883 shortly after his release from prison in Missouri. He confessed shortly before his release.

Robberies attributed to Clarence Hite:

- Winston train, July 1881.
- Blue Cut, train, September 1881.

5. Wood Hite: Robert Woodson Hite born about 1850. Wood was the son of George B. Hite and Nancy James Hite of Logan County, Kentucky. He was the first cousin of Frank and Jesse James. As of 1870 Wood Hite was still living and working on his father's farm in Kentucky. He was killed by Dick Liddil and Bob Ford December 4, 1881 in the home of Martha Bolton, widowed sister of Bob and Charlie Ford. He was reportedly buried in the back yard in a filthy horse blanket.

Robberies attributed to Wood Hite:

- Glendale Missouri, train, October 1879.

- Winston, train, July 1881.

- Blue Cut, train, Missouri September 1881.

6. Frank James: Alexander Franklin James born January 10, 1843 in Missouri, step-son of a doctor turned farmer, Reuben Samuel. He was one of Quantrill's guerrillas. Married Annie Ralston - June 1874, another source says September 1875 in Jackson County, Missouri. Frank had one son Robert Franklin James born February 6, 1878. Frank James died February 18, 1915 *in Missouri and is buried in Independence, Missouri next to his wife Annie Ralston James in the Hill Park Cemetery.*

Robberies attributed to Frank James:

- Liberty, Missouri, bank, 1866.

- Russellville Kentucky, bank, 1868.

- Gallatin Missouri, bank, 1869.

- Corydon Iowa, train, 1871.

- Columbia Kentucky, bank, 1872.

- Saint Genevieve, Missouri, bank, 1872.

- Kansas City, fair box office, 1872.

- Adair Iowa, train, 1873.

- Gad's Hill, Missouri, train, 1874.

- Murder of Pinkerton agent Whicher, 1874.

- Otterville Missouri, train, 1876.

- Northfield Minnesota, bank, 1876.

- Winston, train, July 1881.

- Blue Cut Missouri, train, September 1881.

7. Jesse James: Jesse Woodson James was born September 27, 1847. Jesse joined Quantrill late in 1863, after the Lawrence raid. He was injured badly in the right chest in 1865 while attempting to surrender to the Federals. This injury played a factor both in his potential participation in some robberies as well as identifying him later. Jesse married Zee Mims April 24, 1874. There were two surviving children, Jesse Edwards James and Mary. Zee and Jesse had twins while *living in Tennessee* who did not survive. Jesse was killed April 3, 1882.

Robberies attributed to Jesse James:

- Liberty, Missouri, bank, 1866.

- Russellville Kentucky, bank, 1868.

- Gallatin Missouri, bank, 1869.

- Corydon Iowa, train, 1871.

- Columbia Kentucky, bank, 1872.

- Saint Genevieve, Missouri, bank, 1872.

- Kansas City, fair box office, 1872.

- Adair Iowa, train, 1873.

- Gad's Hill, Missouri, train, 1874.

- Murder of Pinkerton agent Whicher, 1874.

- Otterville Missouri, train, 1876.

- Northfield Minnesota, bank, 1876.

- Winston, train, July 1881.

- Blue Cut Missouri, train, September 1881.

8. Hobbs Kerry: Hobbs Kerry was a raw recruit and was thought none too bright. He was also described as a "crack brained simpleton" by others.

Hobbs Kerry named and gave detailed descriptions of the participants in the Otterville robbery, at which he held the horses. He served two years in prison for the robbery.

Robberies attributed to Hobbs Kerry:

- Otterville Missouri, train, 1876.

9. Dick Liddil: James Andrew Liddil was born on September 15, 1852 in Jackson County, Missouri. He is reputed to have ridden with "Bloody Bill Anderson" but this goes in the disputed column due to his birth date. He served a term in prison for horse theft in 1874 or 1877. He married Mattie Collins. He turned state's evidence and testified against Frank James. He died in Kentucky on July 13, 1901.

Robberies attributed to Dick Liddil:

- Glendale Missouri, train, October 1879.

- Winston, train, July 1881.

- Blue Cut Missouri, train, September 1881.

10. Ed Miller: Edward T. Miller, brother of Clell Miller, born about 1856, son of Moses Miller, a Clay County farmer originally from Kentucky. Ed was shot dead by Jesse James, December 1881.

From another source: According to Clarence Hite, the two argued about stopping to get some tobacco and they bravely agreed to settle it by fighting it out. The duel took place in Jackson or Lafayette County, Missouri. After riding some distance, Ed fired at Jesse and shot a hole through his hat, then Jesse turned and shot him off his horse.

Robberies attributed to Ed Miller:

- Glendale Missouri, train, October 1879.

- Blue Cut Missouri, train, September 1881.

11. Donny Pence: Alexander Doniphan (Donny or Donnie) Pence was born on August 15, 1847 in Clay County, Missouri. He was the son of Adam and Ann Pence of Clay County and brother of Bud Pence. Donny died February 25, 1896 of typhoid fever at Samuels Depot, Nelson County, Kentucky and is buried at Stoner's Chapel Cemetery. He married Sarah Isabel (Belle) Samuels November 10, 1870 at Samuels Depot. She is buried at Stoner's Chapel Cemetery but her tombstone is missing. She was the daughter of Wilson and Martha Samuels. They moved to Nelson County in

1866 after being identified, with brother, Bud, as among those who held up a bank in Liberty, Missouri, in February of 1866.

From 1871, Donny was a respected sheriff or deputy in Kentucky for 30 years. Donny rode with Quantrill. His home at Samuels Depot was believed a haven for Frank and Jesse James. Frank James was among those at his funeral. His obituary mentions no children.

Robberies attributed to Donny Pence:

- Liberty Missouri, bank. 1866.

12. Bill Ryan: Alias Tom Hill was born about 1851 and was Irish. He was tried for Glendale train robbery, then convicted and sentenced to 25 years in prison on October 15, 1881 based on the testimony of Tucker Bassham, a James gang member and participant of the Glendale Missouri train robbery. Bill Ryan released April 15, 1889 but his old habits caught up with him. He reputedly hit a tree limb while riding full gallop and fatally injured himself.

He was reportedly a ruthless and indiscreet member of the James gang, members of which were living in the Edgefield neighborhood. Frank and Jesse James and their families left the Nashville area the day after his arrest.

Robberies attributed to Bill Ryan:

- Glendale Missouri, train, October 1879.

All of this only illustrates that crime does not pay. I wonder how many of the James-Younger Gang wished time and time again while serving their prison terms that they had taken another fork in the road early on and had not turned to robbery and murder as their life's vocation. But it was too late for them. Evil deeds cannot be changed by just wishing it so. Once they had embarked on their journey of crime, they could never undo their choice.

Chapter 28

My Thoughts

What are my thoughts about Frank and Jesse James? It was difficult for me to form any. The sources used interpret the same information differently.

There is very little factual information left to mull over. The best of it is the testimony from the trial of Frank James and from newspapers covering it. Even some of the testimony is suspect. All other factual information has been swallowed by the endless and deep black bog of time that never divulges what it has swallowed. All that is left are myths, legends and folk tales.

But people in Frank and Jesse's line of work don't normally want to leave written accounts of their misdeeds behind to haunt them later.

Some of the sources used take one side of the issue while others take the other. Very few take the middle ground.

What has been presented so far tries to put Frank James at the April 11, 1881 Muscle Shoals payroll robbery. But others sources point out other facts.

I will try to sort through what these sources offer and think it all out and hopefully reach a conclusion.

First of all, the source used from Chapter 27 gives other information that point out the differences in personality between Frank and Jesse James.

Frank James was reported to be always set in a look of fixed repose. Frank did not laugh, was sober, sedate and he was reputed as always a splendid man for ambush or scouting parties.

Jesse James was reported as laughing at many things, was light-hearted, reckless and had a devil may care attitude.

There were two different gangs that Frank and Jesse were reputed belonging to. First, there was the James-Younger Gang who were all members from Confederate guerrilla groups. They had fought together during the Civil War. This was the group referred to in the literature as *The Bushwhackers*. They were use to military type raids and were adept at planning, execution of robberies and having their lines of retreat planned out. They had to trust one another and rely on each other for their lives. They rarely took chances and were seldom reckless. After the Northfield Minnesota bank robbery in 1876, members of the James Younger Gang were all dead, imprisoned or had fled. This was the end of them as an effective outlaw band.

There is no doubt that Frank James participated frequently in the activities of this group of outlaws.

Then there was the James Gang organized primarily, according to some sources used in this work, by Jesse James after Northfield. With few exceptions (possibly Ed Miller), they were all raw recruits and had to learn the art of robbery. Some of them were drunks and braggarts (Whiskey Head Bill Ryan), quarreled among themselves and killed one another on occasion, took chances and committed acts that were not the professional trademarks of the James Younger Gang. A good number of them were captured.

I believe that Frank James participated in few if any of the acts of this later group.

Then there was the manner in which Frank and Jesse reacted differently to life in Nashville, Tennessee after the Northfield, Minnesota robbery.

Frank was older and more settled in his ways and from accounts enjoyed his stay in Nashville. It is my belief that he would have remained there with his wife and child for the rest of his years if he had the choice.

Jesse on the other hand was restless and began organizing his band of outlaws in 1880, using the Hite farm in Adairsville, near Russellville in Logan County, Kentucky as their headquarters. From **"Jesse James, the Last Rebel of the Civil War" by T. J. Stiles, Knopf 2002**, Jesse's misdeeds are outlined. He planned and either executed or tried to execute several robberies in Kentucky and Missouri with Dick Liddil, "Wild Bill" Ryan, Wood and Clarence Hite, Ed Miller and tried to convince the Gang members to have Jim Cummins killed. There were several robberies, or attempted stagecoach robberies, store robberies, and a mine payroll robbery supposedly in Dovey's Store safe. Some of these robberies were successful and some were not.

All the while Jesse was getting more paranoid and mistrustful.

Jesse and Dick Liddil attended horse races in and around Nashville and even in Atlanta.

This source elaborates in the actions of Jesse James but doesn't say anything about Frank James participating in any of this.

In fact, Mrs. Wood Hite testified at Frank James trial in Huntsville, Alabama that Frank was only at their house that one time when fleeing Nashville after "Wild Bill" Ryan's capture.

This source further states that in early 1881, Jesse James, Bill Ryan and another man, probably Wood Hite left the Nashville area and headed south. Jesse had discovered a particularly inviting target, a remote army engineering crew working on the Muscle Shoals canal in northern Alabama.

Then there was the fact that Dick Liddil's testimony was probably influenced by his turning state's evidence to testify against Frank James at the Huntsville, Alabama trial.

W. Stanley Hoole states in **Frank *and Jesse James, And Their Comrades In Crime.*** "Eager for the glory of killing the leader of the world's most notorious bandit band, to say nothing of the handsome reward, Bob Ford secretly met Governor T. T. Crittenden of Missouri in a Kansas City hotel at midnight on January 13, 1882. The politically ambitious governor agreed under pressure to pardon Dick Liddil (who had not long before "come in") provided he turned state's evidence against the James Boys, and to pay traitor Ford $5,000 each (some accounts say $10,000 each) for Jesse and Frank – dead or alive."

From another source, Leland R. Johnson, "**The James Gang In Huntsville**," The Huntsville Historical Review, Vol. 2, April, 1972 Number 2 page 8. Dick Liddil was arrested and brought to Huntsville in 1883 by the United States Marshals. He confessed to being a member of the James Gang, but swore that he was not present at, or party to, the robbery of Alexander Smith at Muscle Shoals. The larceny, he said, was committed by William Ryan, Frank and Jesse James. Liddil was found guilty of complicity in crime, as a member of the gang, but the judge suspended the sentence so Liddil might be returned to Missouri to testify in cases there against other members of the James Gang.

Anyway, Dick Liddil's testimony was discounted at Frank James' 1884 trial in Huntsville and very few people believed very much that he had to say.

So what do I think about all of this? As pointed out earlier, the sources are conflicting. A lot of myths, legends and folk tales are still circulating and believed by many.

There is no doubt in my mind that Dick Liddil sold his soul during the Huntsville trial of Frank James to be relieved of other charges pending against him in Missouri.

Frank James lived for another 30 years as a law abiding citizen after the Huntsville trial.

T. J Stiles, quoted previously, said that Jesse James, Bill Ryan and Wood Hite committed the Muscle Shoals payroll robbery. Perhaps all of the witnesses who could not identify Frank James at his Huntsville trial were merely exercising their civic duty as honest men and good citizens, as well as they could, by not recognizing him as being one of the men who committed the robbery. Frank James may not have been one of the men and they were being as truthful about it as they could be.

Frank James had married a young wife in 1874 or 1875 and had one son Robert Franklin James. Perhaps he was trying to settle down to family life in Nashville and took no part in any robbery after that.

I tend to lean this way. I don't believe that Frank James was part of this robbery. Alabama officials were only trying to convict someone for this robbery and Jesse had been killed, Bill Ryan was serving a 25 year sentence so Frank James was the only probable person left. And he had a bad reputation and a warm body!

There may have been evidence from testimony at the Huntsville trial that would have directly tied Jesse James into the Muscle Shoals payroll robbery had he lived to be tried. First of all, Dick Liddil was quoted as saying that one of the horses used by the group when the group left Nashville before the robbery had a lump on its back. In Thomas Peden's testimony, he also testified that one of the horses used by the three men in his saloon the day of the robbery had a peculiar lump on its back.

Then there is the part of Thomas Peden's testimony that one of the three men had something wrong with a finger. Jesse James was missing the last joint on the third finger on his left hand according to the internet source *The James-Younger Gang: Outlaws.*

But who knows? I realize that I could well be wrong. The fathomless black bog of time has the information but will not give up anything factual and meaningful so only the myths, legends and folk tales remain.

One thing is certainly true though. With Jesse's death and Frank's surrender in 1882 and death in 1915, without any doubt the end of the James Gang was at hand. They had departed this life to meet their maker for final judgment and their reward or punishment.

References

Sources in order of use:

Internet:

Ancestry.com

Familysearch.org

"The Outlaws," James W. Sames III.

United States Department of Veterans Affairs.

Website hosted by **Mr. Donald Greyfield**.

James-Younger Gang website "**James - Younger Gang: Outlaws.**"

Published Sources:

"JESSE AMD FRANK JAMES: DID THEIR LIFE OF CRIME EXTEND INTO THE MUSCLE SHOALS AREA?" Dr. Kenneth R. Johnson, professor Emeritus of History, University of North Alabama.

"CEMETERIES OF EAST LAUDERDALE COUNTY, ALABAMA," FRIENDS OF THE ROGERSVILLE PUBLIC LIBRARY, 1966.

"A Walk Through the Past," William Lindsey McDonald, Bluewater Publications 2003.

Ronald Pettus Archives:

History of Killen, Once Known as Masonville, Ronald and Brenda Pettus, 2002, Chapter 16.

"THE JAMES BOYS RODE SOUTH, FRANK AND JESSE JAMES AND THEIR COMRADES IN CRIME," W. Stanley Hoole, Privately printed 1955.

Newspaper **Montgomery Advertiser** July 25, 1993, several articles by Nick Lackeos.

"Jesse James - The Rabbit Man of Humphrey's County," Raymond W. Thorp, Frontier Times courtesy of Western Publications, May 1965.

"Lauderdale County Alabama, Cops and Robbers - (Mostly Robbers), Frank and Jesse James Robbery in 1881," Compiled April 2004 by Lee Freeman.

"The Huntsville Historical Review," Volume 2 April 1972," **The James Gang in Huntsville**, Number 2, Leland R. Johnson.

Newspaper **"The Nashville Tennessean Magazine,"** February 28, 1971, Article by Max York.

"Jesse James, The Last Rebel of the Civil War," T. J. Stiles, Knopf 2002.

"The James Boys In The Valley," Henry Walker, Athens, November 1966, page 16-17.

Other sources:

Interviews with **Paris A. "Billy Rogers** and archived family mementos.

Index

K

P

Palmer, Cathy, 6, 143
Palmer, John M., 14
Peden, Thomas, 102, 115, 116, 118, 131, 213
Peden, Thomas H., 117, 118, 119
Peden, Tom, 130, 133
Pence, Adam, 207
Pence, Alexander Doniphan, 207
Pence, Ann, 207
Pence, Bud, 14, 207
Pence, Donnie, 13, 14, 17
Pence, Donny, 207
Perry, Joab, 14
Pettus, Ronald, 6, 83, 89, 101, 102, 105, 110, 115
Phillips, William Pierce Gray, 30
Pittman, Dave, 133
Pitts, Charlie, 17
Polly, Lydia, 45
Poor, Mary G., 26, 28
Poor, Mary Polly, 26, 28
Powell, Nancy, 30
Price, Sterling, 11, 137
Puckett, Mary, 98

Q

Quantrill, William Clarke, 12, 13, 14, 16, 107, 202, 203, 205, 208

R

Ralston, Annie, 204
Raney, Donald England, 93
Ransey, Samuel, 33
Riley, Hugh, 89, 102, 115, 133
Rodgers, Mary, 40
Rogers, Benjamin, 45
Rogers, Billy, 2, 49, 55, 62, 67
Rogers, Caroline Elizabeth, 45
Rogers, Cate, 47
Rogers, Catharine, 47
Rogers, Charles Oran, 82, 92
Rogers, Clara, 39, 46, 58, 62, 90
Rogers, Coleman, 44, 47
Rogers, Della, 45
Rogers, Doris, 55
Rogers, Edward, 45
Rogers, Elizabeth Drake, 46
Rogers, Ella, 39, 46, 90
Rogers, Elvira I. James, 68, 69
Rogers, Frances, 47
Rogers, Francis Josephine "Jo", 82, 92
Rogers, Francis Marion "Jack", 45
Rogers, Frank, 139
Rogers, Haywood, 47
Rogers, Ira Norman, 2, 4, 39, 46, 81, 82, 90, 92
Rogers, Isaac, 45
Rogers, James H., 45
Rogers, John, 34, 42, 44, 47, 79
Rogers, John Ira, 82, 92
Rogers, Jonathan T., 34, 42, 79
Rogers, Joseph, 34, 42, 45
Rogers, Joseph, Jr., 34, 42, 79
Rogers, Joseph, Sr., 34, 42, 79
Rogers, Lematine, 45
Rogers, Leona, 39, 81, 90
Rogers, Leona D., 46
Rogers, Lucinda S., 45
Rogers, Lucy, 47
Rogers, Malcolm Coleman "Tobe", 45
Rogers, Marilyn Sue, 82, 93
Rogers, Martha, 34, 42, 79
Rogers, Mary, 47
Rogers, Mary D., 45
Rogers, Mary Elizabeth, 40
Rogers, Mary Nancy, 34, 43, 79
Rogers, Matilda, 47
Rogers, Matilda Hill, 93
Rogers, Matilda M. Hill, 60
Rogers, Mayme, 2, 46
Rogers, Mayme Esther, 4, 39, 81, 90, 93

Bluewater Publications is a multi-faceted publishing company capable of meeting all of your reading and publishing needs. Our two-fold aim is to:

1) Provide the market with educationally enlightening and inspiring research and reading materials.

2) Make the opportunity of being published available to any author and or researcher who desires to be published.

We are passionate about preserving history; whether through the re-publishing of an out-of-print classic, or by publishing the research of historians and genealogists. Bluewater Publications is the Peoples' Choice Publisher.

For company information or information about how you can be published through Bluewater Publications, please visit:

www.BluewaterPublications.com

Also check Amazon.com to purchase any of the books that we publish.

Confidently Preserving Our Past,

Bluewater Publications.com

www.ingramcontent.com/pod-product-compliance
Lightning Source LLC
Chambersburg PA
CBHW080459110426
42742CB00017B/2943